
GROWING UP IN BLACK AND WHITE

A Reckoning of Race and Faith in the Heart of the Mississippi Delta

---

DANNY DODD

In memory of my dear sister, Debbie Couey.

Contents

INTRODUCTION

Writing this book has been an intensely personal journey, a return to the days of my youth that has been both enlightening and challenging. It has been enlightening to see how much has changed. I am now addressing an audience that may struggle to recognize the world of the 1960s & 70s. The challenge has been to faithfully recall the stories I share. No one's memory is infallible—mine included, so I seek your grace if my memory differs from yours. But I hope my story of growing up in the distant world of the Mississippi Delta (and beyond) still resonates in the 21st century. In some ways, we have made significant progress from that distant place, but in other ways, we have not. It is in these areas that I believe my story resonates. Even more so, I believe the Biblical story resonates.

I also hope that my journey to faith that grew up and out of the Mississippi Delta of the 1960s, our struggles to recognize and come to grips with racism then, and most significantly, the instruction and guidance of God's Word concerning this ongoing contentious issue can shed some light upon how to possibly defeat it. I genuinely believe that it *can* be defeated, but *only* through the power and mercy of our Savior, Jesus Christ.

So, thank you for taking the journey back with me by reading this book. It was an era of black and white, from the TV shows we watched to the reality of race. I pray that it will be enjoyable and instructive. May God guide us all never to stop growing in our journey through his grace and truth.

Danny Dodd
North Little Rock, AR

Ole Mose

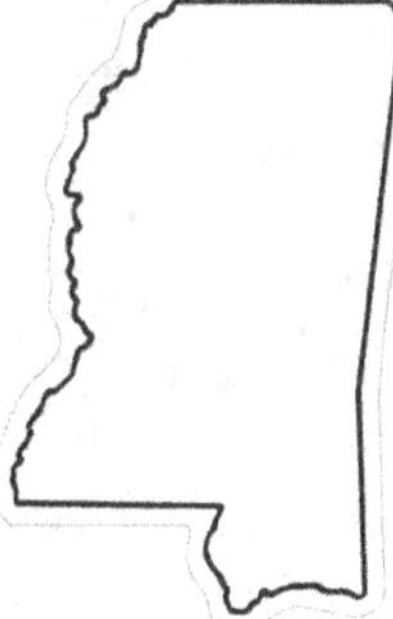

It was one of those steamy, hot Mississippi Delta days—the kind where the humidity seeps deeply into the pores, oppressive and dripping like a steady rainfall. I felt every drop of it rolling off my fresh, buzz-cut head as I hid among the bushes and reeds. Panic was building inside me, for I was convinced I was about to die.

Earlier that day, my pals decided to make a run over the levee to our spot. Everything about Greenville, Mississippi, had to do with the levee in one way or another. It towered above everything—especially from an eight-year-old's perspective who lived in its shadow on South Broadway. It was a silent guard over us, the only thing separating us from the frequent rising waters of the Mississippi River. During the rare winter snowfalls, it became our ski slope. Every Delta kid (and adults, too) grabbed something – anything – to slide down it. In the summer, the levee promised all kinds of adventure—especially on the other side, Lake Ferguson's side. The lake had once been part of the river itself. It was still connected, though, as one of the many oxbow lakes in Mississippi. It indeed was a boy's dream, nothing but pure fun on that side of the levee. My pals, Ray, Stanley, Orange (his given name and the color of his hair), and a boy we called Frog were all older than me, meaning they knew everything. That they let me hang out with them in the summer was more than any kid could ask for. So, when they decided to head over the levee to our spot, I was all in.

Our spot was a wonderful playground of imagination and joy. It was located away from the downtown area of the levee where the boats launched, where the marina was moored, and where folks were always hanging out. It was right on the water, with the surrounding bank area thick with reeds, cane, and brush. A perfect hideout! But what made it, what kept drawing us back like a high-powered magnet, was the old, rusty, beached tugboat. At some point, somehow, this tugboat was parked and forgotten—a relic of bygone days--abandoned to the elements and now to us. We had little doubt that it was our discovery and now ours alone to spend countless hours. We took turns sitting in the decrepit captain's chair, climbing up to the highest deck to serve as a lookout, and pretending to navigate the nearby mighty Mississippi River. We fought off river pirates and Indians and evaded Yankee canons. All while delivering irreplaceable cargo for the Confederacy or to Daniel Boone or wherever our imagination took us. Once we conquered all the dangers of the raging river or got bored—whichever came first—we would retrieve our stashed cane poles, dig up some worms, and catch some bream (pronounced "bre-em"), a freshwater perch, which Lake Ferguson had in abundance. It was all that a kid could hope for!

But on this day, we discovered more. As we ditched our bikes at the bottom and scrambled over the levee near our spot, we first caught a glimpse of him. Getting closer by practicing the silent-Indian-stalking methods that we had seen in our favorite Western TV shows, he came into full view. He was a giant of a man, but not just any man—a black man! And there he was, sitting on a turned-over bucket, fishing in our spot. At first—speaking only for myself—I was a little afraid. After all, it was the 1960s, and what I had heard about black men was enough to frighten anyone. But my pals seemed more agitated than scared. Who did this guy think he was to be fishing in *our spot?* How could we tugboat down the river with him there? This was supposed to be our secret, after all. So, we (I say "we," but it was really "they") devised a plan.

Long before we had discovered that certain reeds made excellent spears when pulled out of the Delta gumbo soil.

The gumbo that clodded up on the end of the reed when yanked up out of the earth gave it enough weight to be thrown a fair distance only occasionally accurately. It also fit rather nicely into our momentary alignment with our imagined Indian heritage. Chunking spears just seemed to follow stalking. It was decided then. We would get our reed/gumbo spears and let that interloper have it. No one —let alone a black guy—was going to usurp our preordained spot.

Now, as kids do, none of us thought beyond that unfortunate decision. We were in the moment, and the moment owned us. Gathering false courage from one another, we launched. I believe Ray fired first (he was our leader), then the other boys, and then me. I maybe threw one weak and wobbly spear (I was still scared but trying not to show it). And I do recall that as the spears were flung, some words were flung with them. One in particular—what we now identify as the "N-word."

THAT WORD

That word was ever so common in my formative years. Almost everyone, who was white anyway, used it. One exception was my maternal grandmother—Ma Whit. Her name was Vallie Whittington, but she was Ma Whit to almost everyone. She was a grand 'ole southern lady. She was the perfect picture of a grandmother: sweet, kind, and generous. She loved Elvis Presley and professional wrestling (later, I would argue that it was fake, but she would have none of it). She had beautiful white hair and a gracious smile. I don't recall hearing that word from her. Instead, she used gentler terms. But aside from her, though, it was the N-word for sure. That sounds shocking and scandalous now. For Ray, Orange, Stanley, and Frog to shout it out was, unfortunately, a result of our environment and conditioning. Thankfully, that word has now been outed for what it always was—offensive, repulsive, and dehumanizing, but things were different back then. There were many variations and usages of that word to describe numerous things associated with black people, which were all demeaning and cruel, but all sprinkled throughout everyday conversation then. I grew up hearing this and, sadly, what I said myself until one day earlier that summer.

Ray's family lived in one of those big leftover stately brick homes on Broadway, our street. This home was a remnant of more prosperous times, possessing a sense of faded glory, but still quite impressive to me, a boy just processing such things. It had huge (to me, anyway) dingy white columns surrounding the spacious front porch. There were large rooms, a fireplace, high ceilings with squeaky old fans, and definitely a sense that somebody significant had once lived there. It is where we all hung out when we were not over the levee. Plus, Ray's family had a maid.

If you have ever seen *The Help*, you can get the idea. Her name was Flora. She was a rather round and sweet black lady who was always pleasant and patient with us boys despite often causing her more work. I probably never thought much about Flora as a kid up to this point. She was just there doing what she did. She would happily (it seemed anyway) get us cookies and milk as we watched TV. Then, one day, things changed —at least for me.

An old game show was playing—*Truth Or Consequences*. I cannot recall why that captured our attention on that day. The host was long-time TV personality Bob Barker, and we boys were gathered up close to the television and were really into it. On this particular day, one of the contestants just happened to be black, which was a rarity then, and we were rooting for her to win. I remember it vividly. As she was struggling to come up with the correct answer to win the grand prize, I blurted out (as if she could hear me) encouragement for her to guess correctly—and I used the N-word. Yep, without even hesitating. Almost immediately, though, instinctively, I turned to Flora, who was ironing clothes in the back of the room. The hurt in her eyes and the pain on her face were evident even to an eight-year-old boy. I felt a wave of shame sweep over me. Despite the everyday use of that word, I knew it was wrong to have said it. I tried to stammer out an apology to her. She played it off like it was no big deal (no doubt conditioned to do so), but the experience changed me even at that young age, I decided to try hard not to use that word again.

Back to the man who had invaded our space. The other boys had no such epiphany, and as the spears flew— so did that word. And then it went all predictably sideways. As the spears crashed down around the man and into the water (I do not think any of our "ammunition" actually hit him), he turned and let out a yell! He stood up to reveal himself to be at least as large as a grizzly bear to our bulging eyes. Then he started toward us. Everyone scattered. To this day, I still do not know where the other boys went or how they escaped so quickly. All I know is that they vanished—leaving me to dive into the brush and reeds, trying desperately to dig out a hiding place in the gumbo and scared out of my mind, knowing that if discovered, I likely was breathing my last of that hot, sticky Delta air.

A TINY CRACK IN THE WALL

However, there was little chance of my not being discovered, and soon, this giant was standing before me!

Sweating profusely in his white t-shirt and blue work pants, he looked down at me. Any fleeting hope that he did not see me was shattered when he boomed, "Come on out of there, white boy." I was so frightened I could not move, so I remained paralyzed, praying he would go away. No such luck. He repeated, "Come on up out of there, NOW." Somehow, I managed to swallow my heart that had moved up into my throat—enough anyway to mutter something like, "I am sorry, please don't hurt me." After all, I knew all of the stories of a big black man snatching away white children who strayed too far from home and had already convinced myself that this was the guy! When he heard my feeble, whimpering voice, he just let out a whistle and proclaimed, "I ain't gonna hurt you, boy. Even if I was a mind to, that would just mean the end of me." (I did not know what he meant then, but I do now.) Then he reached down his massive hand to help me out. It was the most enormous hand I had ever seen! I briefly imagined that if he closed it up in a fist, it would be the same size as a sledgehammer. I hesitated but finally took it and, with his help, scrambled out of my hasty hiding place.

He peered down at me and said, "Folk call me Ole Mose (pronounced Moz). What is your name, son?" This threw me off guard. We had just basically bombarded him —ruined his fishing and potentially injured him—yet here he was introducing himself and not killing me? With my heart still pounding, I told him my name when I recovered enough to remember it. He motioned for me to follow him and sit near where he had been fishing. Then he got around to it—asking me why we had done such a thing to him, how he was minding his own business, trying to catch a few fish for supper, and how that was not any way to treat anyone. And why in the world had we used that shameful word? It was a hurtful word. That it just wasn't right to call a fella that.

I may have attempted to say something about this being our spot, about our tugboat, that we were just being Indians, etc., but what I really remember was the grace of Ole Mose. Here was this immense black man—the man of the frightening legends—being kind and generous to me. As he finished his talk, he did something even more surprising. He suggested that we become friends and that if ever, on occasion, we wanted to tugboat down the river at the same time he was fishing, he would consent to us and leave us to it—just no more wild Indians and spears. I agreed and promised to talk to my pals. Then we shook hands on it (or rather, my hand disappeared into his), and both went on our way with me still on shaky legs and thankful to still be alive. And that was that.

But it wasn't. I have never forgotten Ole Mose. My friends agreed, and we encountered him a few more times at our spot that summer. He always offered to leave, but we never felt right about it after what we did. He may even have gotten a kick or two overhearing our tugboat adventures. We even fished with him once or twice. I never saw him again after that summer, nor did I ever tell anyone in my family about him—it was still the Mississippi Delta in the 1960s. However, I can still see him blocking the sun over me, reaching out that gentle, gigantic hand. More than just a memory of a brief summer encounter, Ole Mose continues to impact me.

Ole Mose started my thinking that not everything I heard was necessarily true; that just because skin had a different pigment tone, that was nothing to fear. I had a long way to go (and still do in many ways), but looking back, my experience with Ole Mose first taught me (although, at such a young age, I had yet to understand fully) that dignity, acceptance, and even friendship should know no color. There on the banks of Lake Ferguson that hot summer in the heart of the Mississippi Delta, I learned a life lesson that perhaps I could not have learned the same way anywhere else—it should be the character of a person that matters most, not the color of the skin on the outside.

Ole Moss represented the first tiny crack for me in that great wall that separated black from white. It was an invisible wall, but it was a wall nonetheless with rules both written and embedded in law and unwritten that were designed to keep us apart, keep suspicion and fear alive, and keep equality for black people at bay. I grew up on the white side of that wall, and at eight years old, I was not yet old enough to process it all. Ole Moss knew about that wall. He lived on the other side. Yet, for a brief moment during that summer, I experienced the first cracks in that wall because of him. Those cracks would grow greater and greater, and not just for me. Thankfully, that old wall is mostly gone, but other walls, taller and thicker since been erected, to take its place—different kinds of walls, to be sure, but still there to overcome.

MEMORIES AND MORE:

- Cane pole fishing was the standard mode of angling then in the Mississippi Delta. You could fashion your own out of the local cane or purchase one, relatively inexpensively, that had been treated and would last longer. It was basically a long, strong, but flexible stick with a fishing line attached. There was nothing like whipping that line out in the water (which was a learned art), watching and waiting for the bobbing cork to be jerked underwater by a monster bream. Then the fight was on! Worms and crickets were the preferred bait. Almost every Delta boy worth his salt found pride in the dirty hands produced by handling this bait. Almost every Delta girl would not consider touching such "yucky" creatures.

- Summers seemed different then than now. Maybe it is nostalgia, but the pace was slower. Fishing, swimming, summer league baseball games, riding bicycles, reading comics, and looking for old soda pop bottles filled our time. School did not start until Tuesday after Labor Day, so we had a full three months to enjoy. It was a joyous time to be a kid.

- *Truth or Consequences* was the first game show ever broadcast on television—shifting over from the radio. It ran in some form on TV from the early 50s through the late 80s. Contestants on the show were asked trivia questions. If they failed to produce the correct answer, they would face the consequence, usually participating in some type of silly stunt. It eventually evolved into a more traditional game show when hosted by Bob Barker. Of course, he would move on from this show to become instantly recognizable as the host of *The Price is Right.*

- Daniel Boone loomed large in my childhood. To my buddies and me, he was a true American hero. Of course, the popular TV show about him in the late 60s and early 70s starring the rugged actor Fess Parker fed into our idolization of the frontiersman. As I will mention later, coonskin caps were the height of fashion for the cool kids in Greenville during this time. And if we could not play the role of Daniel, being Mingo, his trusted Native American sidekick, was equally desired. In adulthood, I have reacquired a genuine "Fess Parker as Daniel Boone" coonskin cap along with a Mingo rubber tomahawk. We kids knew how to roll back in the day!

- I never heard much of anything about racism, per se, as a young child. It was not discussed. Things were simply as they were and had been that way for so long that most folks just accepted it—at least most white folks. And most of these weren't terrible people; they did not hate; they were not unkind, but the wall did its job, and life went on as it had without many questioning the injustice until the burden the wall was holding up could no longer bear the pressure anymore.

2

Greenville, Mississippi

The Greenville of my growing-up years was an enchanted place to me. It was called the Queen City of the Delta. It was known as the home of a Pulitzer Prize winner, progressive-minded, and even somewhat cosmopolitan—a surprising ethnic melting pot. Overall, it was a thriving, vibrant small city. But as a boy growing up there, I was unaware of any of that, nor would it even have mattered. I just knew it offered fun and adventure on many levels.

There was the levee—always the levee with the lake on the other side. It is difficult to convey to anyone unfamiliar with life by a levee how significant this long stretch of artificial mountain could be. It protected us, and it gave us the lake. From imagined tugboat adventures to real fishing trips with my father and grandfather, it was all a boy's life needed. I grew up on that lake at first catching those ubiquitous bream by the dozens, then later graduating to the elusive largemouth bass as I mimicked every cast and threw every lure like my angling hero, TV fisherman Bill Dance. Our go-to fishing destinations were Lake Ferguson, nearby Lake Lee, and surrounding bar-pits. Bar-pits were giant holes carved out of the earth when the land was excavated to make the levee, which filled up with water and fish. They were ours to explore, and we did. Untold hours were spent fishing and hunting on the other side of the levee.

THE PARAMOUNT THEATER

Yet there was more. There was this magical downtown street—Washington Avenue. I am not sure that even Hollywood could capture the allure of that street and what it meant to a young boy. Everything was on that street! Just strolling down it was like a holiday, especially when it was the holidays. One particular block stood at the intersection of my life—where Washington Avenue and Broadway met. On it was the majestic Paramount Theater, which had grand architecture and an intimidating stage. It was built for Broadway productions, and had incredible balconies and box seats. Many a Saturday afternoon was spent there escaping into the delightful matinees—everything from John Wayne westerns to the latest from Disney. Even now, I can imagine catching a whiff of the inviting aroma of their buttered popcorn while scarfing down some Milk Duds and watching young cartooned King Arthur strain until he pulls the sword from the stone—wonderful, carefree days.

The Paramount was also the scene of a colossal heartbreak for me. Regularly, the theater ran promotions, including drawings for prizes of all kinds. Typically, it was associated with a soft drink brand—RC Cola, Barq's Root Beer, or the then-new sensation Mountain Dew. One of my fondest memories was securing one of those early promotional hillbilly Mountain Dew felt hats. I cherished it almost as much as my Daniel Boone coonskin cap.

One of my older cousins had won a brand-new sparkling Ford Mustang at one of the Paramount promotional giveaways. That was truly unbelievable! So, as you might expect, I came to believe it was a family entitlement that I win something at least equally as grand.

Every Saturday that rolled around offered another chance to fulfill my destiny—and in storybook fashion, on one Saturday, I did. My ticket was drawn. My number was announced. It was my foreordained day! As I floated toward that vast stage, all of its intimidation evaporated. My mind was racing with the possibilities! It had to be at least a bike. But maybe it was a car! I would have preferred a Jeep or perhaps something even better whatever that could be! But sadly, it was not to be. My whole world came crashing down in a heap as I was given my prize—a Baby Ruth candy bar! I was positive that a mistake had been made. I wanted to peek behind one of those huge curtains; surely my Jeep was back there. It had to be a joke or something—a candy bar! No way was this possible. But it was. All my extremely high hopes were dashed as I slunk back to my seat only to collapse in tears to my sister, Dottie. As wonderful as Greenville was and as fairytale-like as the Paramount seemed, they both disappointed me that day in a significant way.

It never occurred to me that it was disappointing to others as well, and not just on that day. The "colored" (another word regularly used when talking about black people) was still regulated to those balconies. Even winning a Baby Ruth back then was out of their reach. Of course, as I threw myself a huge pity party at that moment, I was utterly oblivious to this reality. Still, it was always there— that invisible wall so often separating us.

WASHINGTON AVENUE

Back to Washington Avenue. On one side of the Paramount was the neatest little store that, in my mind, ever existed—the Marion Parlor. It was a sort of drugstore that sold a little bit of everything, even offering a soda fountain and hamburgers. Included on their shelves was, some rather unique merchandise I found utterly irresistible— items like onion gum, fake vomit, exploding pens, hand buzzers, and other fascinating novelties. It became an ongoing goal to find enough empty soda bottles, cash them in, and save all that money to purchase one of these treasures. To see some unwitting soul pop onion gum into their mouth only to twist up their face in shock as the unexpected sourness overtook their palate was worth every torturous minute spent searching for bottles. What more could a kid hope for?

THE MAGIC OF CHRISTMAS

Greenville offered still more. Just beyond the Paramount on that block was the massive, two-story Sears and Roebuck store. The second floor housed all of the toys, and at Christmastime, it was turned into the grandest winter wonderland known worldwide, complete with visits from Santa himself. His big red-and-green detailed chair would be entrenched in the middle of a massive display of lavishly decorated and lighted Christmas trees with cute little Christmas trains continually chugging around them, next to samples of the latest, most incredible toys, directly from the North Pole. That setting mesmerized me. I would stand captivated, completely lost in time while soaking it all in and dreaming of seeing those toys under my own Christmas tree. My dad was a city fireman, but he also worked at Sears on his off days. Delightfully, that gave him the inside track on those toys: G.I Joe, Mattel's Shootin Shell cap gun and holster, the Marx Toy Company's Johnny West, Chief Cherokee, Fort Apache playset, and the Battleground set. I eagerly awaited Christmas morning and dreamed of what Santa and Sears had for me. It made me gloriously happy.

It wasn't just Sears, though. Next to it was Kress Five and Dime. It, too, drew me in, as we say in the South, like a fly on a watermelon. Kress had what no other store could ever hope to match. They had Santa's actual footprints—starting on the sidewalk in front of the store, continuing through the store, past display after display of toys, and leading directly to Santa surrounded by elves! (Even now, thinking about this set-up and the welcome anticipation generated by walking in those white footsteps makes my heart flutter.) It never occurred to me to inquire how Santa could do his gig at Sears and Kress simultaneously, plus manage all of his load back in the home office at the North Pole. All I knew was pure, euphoric Christmas joy—the kind only a kid can experience.

At the other end of Washington Avenue, down by the WWII memorial sign, by the levee end, was a true Greenville institution—Stein Mart. In its own way, it, too, was a wonderland. The Steins were a pillar of the city. They were Russian Jewish immigrants who made good through hard work and genius. Merchants from way back created this one-of-a-kind store. Both my mother, Eleanor (for a time), and my aunt, "Ma Rose" (for a long time), worked there—the first and original Stein Mart. The store was known for getting leftovers, seconds, and other unsold clothing items from places like Sax Fifth Avenue in New York City and selling them in Greenville at discounted prices. Nearly everyone went to Stein Mart. Who would not want to wear clothes from fancy New York stores? The Steins certainly outfitted me. That was for sure.

Perhaps, though, Washington Avenue may have been most famous—at least to me then—because of its Christmas parade from one end of it to the other. Words fail me to describe the wonderment of it all adequately. Christmas lights strung along the street. The storefronts were gayly decorated for the season. The Christmas spirit in the air. It was magical. Wow. From various marching bands to Shriners buzzing around in tiny cars to one beautiful float after another to horses proudly strutting, to finally Santa himself tossing out wave after wave of candy. It was almost as eagerly anticipated as Christmas morning itself.

THE OTHER SIDE OF THE STREET

Behind all of this joy, during much of my young boyhood, was the fact that all of this Washington Avenue wonder was mainly enjoyed by those with white faces. The invisible wall created a proverbial "other side of the street" for black people. Again, I was unaware of this segregation as a youngster. Perhaps black folks had their own celebration along Nelson Street (the main thoroughfare in the black business district in town), but it was never discussed, and by the time of my teen years, much had changed. Then, one of the highlights of the Washington Avenue Christmas Parade was the Mean Green Marching Machine—the Mississippi Valley State University Delta Devils band from tiny Itta Bena, Mississippi. MVSU is a historically black university. Their high-stepping, energizing routine was as much art and dance as it was marching. Standing in front of Stein Mart, which was our custom, we could see them coming long before we heard them due to the swell in the crowd on the sidewalks following them as they performed. They brought smiles to every face. Yet, almost without fail, I would hear someone ridicule them using various racial slurs. It was the mid-70s, and racial progress had been made, but not everyone went along for the ride.

DELTA DEMOCRAT TIMES

Earlier, I mentioned that Greenville was home to a Pulitzer Prize winner. That would have been Hodding Carter, Sr. He was a trail-blazing newspaperman who, for years, helmed the *Delta Democrat Times*, which was Greenville's daily newspaper. He was slightly before my time but was a legendary figure. I attended Greenville public schools with his granddaughters, Catherine and Finn, who I secretly crushed on but were out of my league. Their father, Hodding, Jr., was the paper's publisher as I grew up. Later, he became President Jimmy Carter's press secretary. Finn went off to Hollywood to star in movies like *Tremors*. The senior Carter, followed by his son, led the way for Greenville to become the first city in Mississippi to desegregate its schools. He was known to push a progressive agenda on racial issues. To many, he was a hero. To others, not so much. I can recall often hearing the newspaper criticized and dismissed by using harsh, racially-tinted language. However, it was because of that kind of leadership that Greenville made progress on racial equality before other Mississippi cities. As I witnessed, while tensions continued to exist between the races, Greenville did not experience the kinds of infamous blatant racial violence that marred other Mississippi communities in the 1960s.

Hodding Carter, Sr. was but one of the many Greenville literary notables. Others, such as Alexander Percy, Walker Percy, Ellen Douglas, Beverly Lowery, Ben Keating, and Shelby Foote, called Greenville their home. At times, Greenville enjoyed a sophistication well beyond its limits and location in the heart of the Delta.

A SURPRISING MELTING POT

Greenville was a true melting pot. The Steins were representative of a healthy Jewish population. Years before, Italian immigrants had settled in Greenville, and their descendants were integrated into the town's life. There was a large Chinese contingency, with several establishing grocery stores, which were dotted all around the city. One such store flourished in my neighborhood, located just off of South Broadway—Lucky Food Store.

My growing-up address was 712 South Broadway. No one would have ever described it as a destination location. South Broadway had seen its better years, and while it boasted a few impressive older homes (like Ray's), they were aging out. We were not poor but far from being among Greenville's elite. Our address alone demonstrated that. I lived in an old, rambling home next to my uncle's house, encircled by the same fence. At one point, my grandmother, Ma Whit, lived in our house in an early form of a mother-in-law suite. Later, she moved nearby in another house, of course, on Broadway. My dad was a fireman. My uncle was a policeman. Life centered around Broadway. A few blocks up from our house toward downtown and Washington Avenue was Ella Darling Elementary School. All three of my older sisters and not a few cousins were schooled there ahead of me, and when my time came, off I went as well.

One big difference, however, was that most of my school time was spent integrated. I cannot recall attending school without black children. But not just black, but Italian, Jewish kids, and Chinese too. It was just life as I knew it. I even had—if ever so briefly—a black girlfriend. Back then, it was all carefree. You would simply ask a girl to be your girlfriend. If she said "yes," then it was official. We truthfully had no clue what it meant, only that all the big kids did it. My brief fling with Rene ended about as quickly as it started. One day, I teased her on the playground by calling her "Grenade." She promptly cracked me over the head with a stick, and off I ran, crying to the teacher. We were blissfully unaware of how scandalous such a real relationship would be.

This was the Greenville of my youth—amazing and

wonderful but also perplexing. It was a city of progress but also of limitations, especially in terms of race. It was like a child trying to mature but hampered by an imbalanced, incomplete diet. Some attempted to tear down the wall, while others were working to keep it propped up. One scene perfectly illustrates this to me. It happened at Lucky Food Store.

LUCKY FOOD STORE

Lucky was my store. Right around the corner from my house, it was my destination for everything a kid needed. I cashed in my precious cache of empty soda bottles there. It was my go-to for comics (Superman, Batman, Spiderman, and Archie), ice cream, candy, and an Orange Crush soda anytime I could afford them. The Chinese owners always treated me kindly, except when we would get too animated over the new comics. Then, we were encouraged to quiet down and not disturb the adult customers. As much as I enjoyed trips to this store on one visit, I wished I was some-where else.

Not too far from our little Broadway world was a predominately black neighborhood with Clay Street as its main artery. There were many days when my sisters, cousins, and I journeyed the length of Clay Street on foot to get to Greenville's public swimming pool, unaware and unconcerned about the optics of being little white kids walking through a black neighborhood. There were never any problems. Increasingly, some of the residents of Clay Street and the surrounding area chose Lucky's for their grocery shopping.

And on that day—just like me—one black lady prob-ably wished she were somewhere else. It all started over an accusation that this lady took an item from another

woman's—a white lady's—basket. I remember the shout-
ing, anger, that word being used, and the awfulness of it
all. And I remember faces—the anger and hatred in the
white face and the hurt, resentment, and tears on the black
woman's. As I stood there with my candy in hand,
witnessing this confrontation, I was stunned and confused.
As I recall, the Chinese owners put squarely in the middle
of this mess believed the black woman's denial of wrong-
doing, and why not? Why would anyone swipe a food item
from someone's cart when all they had to do was get their
own off the shelf? But after a prolonged rant, including
threats to call the authorities, the Chinese owners caved
and asked the black lady to leave. They felt the pressure,
too, no doubt heightened by the reality of having to do
business during that time. They realized which side of the
wall held the power. Better not to offend the white population, I suppose.

ALWAYS WITH ME

This was just a snapshot of the struggle—Greenville's
growing pains. Fundamental, lasting changes eventually
did arrive, and I was around to experience a brief
moment, but it came perhaps too late. Greenville is no
longer the city of my boyhood. White flight occurred,
followed by people from all of those ethnic groups escaping
the long-term economic downturn. Factories and industries fled, seeking to pay lower wages elsewhere. The Paramount was demolished to make room for a parking lot.
That old spacious Stein Mart is gone as well—now with a
little plaque there to remember what once was, as a new
courthouse is being constructed on that location. The
Sears and Kress stores long ago ceased to be. Not much on
Washington Avenue remains as it was from those bygone

days except for Jim's Café—now a city landmark. (If you ever get to Greenville, stop by to get an authentic taste of the Delta.) The city now looks old and forlorn, with, ironically, the former Uncle Ben's Rice Factory (now renamed Ben's Original) remaining as one of the last large industries in town.

Nevertheless, Greenville will always be the sparkling city of my childhood. A city that, in some ways, was ahead of its time but also could never fully overcome larger forces at play. Much of what I now am comes from that city. Its tensions became my tensions. As it struggled to face the ugly reality of racism, so did I—to face down the realities of that wall. As it incrementally progressed in that area, so did I. Greenville may not be what it once was, but it remains home in all kinds of ways. No matter where life takes me, Delta Gumbo has a way of sticking to the toes.

MEMORIES AND MORE:

- In my circle back then, Bill Dance was the guy we all wanted to grow up to be. Fishing all of the time and being paid to do so! Amazing! Sign me up! We tuned into every episode of *Bill Dance Outdoors*. We could sing the introduction song. He taught us all to bass fish. We all wanted an orange and white University of Tennessee cap like he wore (I purchased an autographed one as an adult. I still have it!). Such was his influence on us.
- I still enjoy going to the movies. It is one of the things my daughters and I still do together. I can trace that back to the Paramount. It truly

was magical to a young kid. The phrase, "They
don't make them like they used to," applies to
that grand ole palace. Entering it was like
entering another world with its ornate features,
balconies, and old-school luxury that all worked
together to make going to a movie an event, at
least for a portion of the population.
Hollywood came alive there.

- Marx toys. This company was started by Louis
  Marx and his brother David in 1919 and grew
  to be the largest toy manufacturer in the world
  during the mid-twentieth century, creating
  legendary items such as Rock-em Sock-em
  Robots and the Big Wheel tricycle. They had
  everything any self-respecting boy could
  imagine. I spent countless hours with their
  products—riding the western range with the
  movable cowboy Johnny West and his horse,
  Thunderbolt; winning WWII all over again in
  their Battlefield playset (the German toy
  soldiers and equipment were gray. The US
  troops and gear was green); and launching
  rockets into space with their Cape Canaveral
  set. The details in these toys were incredible. I
  have recollected some of these toys as an adult.
  It is pure nostalgia offering me a chance if just
  for a fleeting moment to feel like that wide-
  eyed, innocent young Delta boy again.
- Soda was a big part of my youth, except we
  never called it "soda." We appropriated the
  Coca-Cola brand and called all soft drinks
  "cokes" in the generic sense. But we all had our
  favorites. Mine included Orange Crush in the
  brown bottles. Another favorite was Barq's

(pronounced "barks") Root Beer. Greenville
had a local bottling plant—the same with
Mountain Dew. I even went there as a child to
see the bottling process, which was captivating
for a kid. "Yahoo! Mountain Dew!" was their
catchphrase. I enjoyed Nehi Grape Soda as
well. My sisters were all about Dr. Pepper. It
was the drink then to enjoy at ten, two and four
o'clock, so the advertisement went. I recall how
they put peanuts into their bottles. Empty soda
bottles were equally as important as full ones.
We would get "good money" for them at stores
like Lucky's. If we had a bottle to cash in, we
could reduce the price of a new bottle of Coke
to eight cents. Imagine that.

- I did experience a fully integrated school
  system. White, black, Italian, Chinese, and
  Jewish all coexisted with little turbulence.
  Somehow we all managed to get along. I think
  if we could do it then, we should be able to do
  it now.

3

"We Shall Overcome"

Washington Avenue on the levee end, the Stein Mart block, was typically busy. The Downtowner, once the elite hotel of Greenville, was just across the street. People were always scurrying around doing day-to-day typical business. I thought this day was no different as I approached the entrance to Stein Mart to visit my mom. The occasion for me to do so was early dismissal at my school, Ella Darling —giving us a wonderful afternoon free. The sun was brightly shining, illuminating the Delta sky, and life was good for a kid who had unexpectedly escaped the prison of school. So, I decided to enjoy that freedom by walking down my favorite street, popping into stores to check on the latest from Marx Toys, and then to see Mom and my aunt at work. The closer I got to Stein Mart, however, I came to realize that this was not going to be an ordinary day. There was a larger-then-normal crowd gathered. Some folks seemed a bit frustrated or even angry. Then, beyond them, I began to realize why.

A group of black people were in front of Stein Mart. They had signs, were walking in a circle, and singing. I could see determination and resolve combined with a touch of fear on their faces. Courageously, they marched, not dissuaded by the onlookers. There was crowd noise, but I made out the song, *We Shall Overcome Some Day*. Confused, I tried to understand what was happening. Then I became nervous. I could feel the tension in the air. At that time, I noticed a police presence with my uncle among them. They, too, were observing, either there to prevent tensions from becoming trouble or in case they did. But they didn't—thankfully. So, finding an opening, I waved to my uncle and entered the store to see my mom.

But I remained perplexed. Never had I seen this before, and I was unsure why it was happening. I asked my mom, but she did not have the time to discuss it on the job. I remember it all being quite bothersome. Why were these folks carrying those signs and singing? Why did other people seem angry about it? What were they trying to overcome? I determined to find some answers, so I went to the one person I could talk to—my grandmother.

MA WHIT

I've mentioned Ma Whit. She, indeed, was the matriarch of our family. She had fled the economic hardscrabble times of the Mississippi hill country before WWII to find better employment in Greenville, the Queen City of opportunity. Widowed since my mother was five and with two sons also to rear, she was a Renaissance woman. She worked several different jobs—one of which was the matron for the women's city jail. She never achieved much financially, but her legacy still shapes my family today. She was gentle but also tough. A fabulous cook who, born of the depression hardships, never wasted any scrap of food. If nothing else, those scraps found their way into her unparalleled tomato-based vegetable soup. She was the person to whom we all turned for advice and answers. That is why I trusted her to calm the frustrations I took to her that day.

THE WALL WAS CHALLENGED

At this point in life, I became more aware of life beyond Greenville. There were larger forces at play in the world. I became more aware of the racial tension outside my little Broadway bubble. Even so, the downtown demonstration was so unexpected and new to me. Ma Whit would help me figure it out. One thing that stood out in my memory as she spoke with me was her language. Her words were compassionate and gentle. She spoke graciously about black people. She explained how this group was protesting against mistreatment and other unfair obstacles they faced. She told me that the song they sang was an old gospel hymn representing overcoming oppression. She assured me that it was okay, as long as it was done peacefully, and that she hoped things could change for them. I was encouraged not to hang around the protests, just in case something happened, but as long as my uncle was there, she did not worry too much. She shared this kindly and patiently, which was enough for me. I don't recall asking her any further questions except for one. Why were they doing it now?

I'll never forget her answer. "Dr. Martin Luther King," she replied. This was one name that had penetrated my little protected existence. I was aware that he was a preacher—a black preacher who was creating all sorts of havoc for some across the South. I had caught glimpses of him on TV news as my parents watched it. I had over-heard a talk about him. Primarily, I had heard that he was a troublemaker, trying to stir up the blacks against the whites. He was a threat to the wall. And I remember, on one occasion, someone saying something more pointed than that.

We were at the Fireman's Lodge. This was a house on the wonderful other side of the levee. It was on the banks of Lake Ferguson, and the Greenville firefighters and their families had access. Growing up, I went with my father, our family, and other firefighter's family to enjoy cookouts, hang out, and, most of all, fish. It was located on the oppo-site end of the lake from our beached tugboat. Like that hideout, it offered fun and adventure, too. Instead of a tugboat, an old rotting river barge was embedded behind the lodge in the lake's bank. It was half-submersed and offered inviting fishing opportunities—especially for the easily caught bream. They would bed up within the submerged parts of that old barge. We would catch them through the rotted parts of the deck on our cane poles using crickets as bait. It was a blast, but it was also dangerous. Every trip onto the barge was proceeded by the be-careful speech. "Watch out for those holes." "If you fall in, we will never be able to find you." But a boy tends to forget that once caught up in the excitement of fishing. Sure enough, during one trip, I became so enthralled while watching my dad catch a fish that I stepped backward into one of those holes! Thankfully, I managed to grab the deck before disappearing forever into the dark brown muddy water. After a few screams, I was retrieved, hugged, dried off, then scolded. Afterward, I went right back to fishing.

It was at this lodge that I overheard the talk about Dr. King. I have no idea what was spoken, but one sentence remains etched in my mind. One of the men there starkly stated, "Somebody ought to do something about that N..." Well, sadly, somebody eventually tragically did.

I was at Ma Whit's house when the news broke of Dr. King's assassination. Unfortunately, this was not the first of my lifetime, but it did mark the first time I started to grasp how truly ugly and incredibly horrible hate is. Even growing up as I did with all of the racial overtones, I had not equated it all to hate, harm, or injury. All of that was present but not yet real to me. Even with the use of that word, the idea of actually harming someone because they were a different color never entered my mind. I was just too young to connect all the dots. But with the murder of Dr. King, I became much more aware of the violence, suspicion, anger, hatred, and fear that always seem to go hand-in-hand with racism.

My grandmother took the news hard. Her immediate

reaction was fear. She was afraid this would spark race riots. My uncle and all other Greenville police personnel were put on full alert. She was also sorrowful. She cried. I believe she cried over his loss of life and also over what she thought it would ignite. I was set to head out to Lucky's to pick up some new comic books before the breaking news, but she would not allow me to leave. Too dangerous now, she warned.

As it turned out, there were no race riots in Greenville. We joined the rest of the world monitoring the news as it continued to report about his murderer and the ongoing consequences of his death. I could not help but think of the Stein Mart demonstrators—wondering if they would continue to sing, "We shall overcome" after such a significant blow. This indeed became an event that shaped me and caused me to become more alert and aware of the prevalence of racism and the damage it creates. It aided me in recognizing the reality of that invisible wall and the damage it does. But it was not the only event.

CATCHING CATFISH

It was another of those oppressively humid Delta summers as I was about to enter my teen years. Thanks to my sister, Debbie, I had snagged a job working with a commercial fisherman on the Mississippi River. Finally, I could fully venture out of Lake Ferguson and onto the river to explore it just as we had imagined on the tugboat years before. Catching catfish from dawn to dusk! I was pumped! The reality, however, turned out to be quite different. It became more like cleaning catfish from dawn until dusk. It wasn't really fishing; it was more like work. Sure, there were some memorable adventures. Mr. Strait, the fisherman, had an ancient wooden boat with a deep-V hull. It was an old monster, but it could handle the river currents. He enjoyed falling in behind the river tugboats, hanging out in their wakes, bouncing around, waving at the guys on the barges, and laughing about it all. I did not always accompany him, but when I did, it was exciting running the trot lines to see if we had snagged a "biggun" (that is what we called a large fish of any type). But typically, for me, it was about baiting the hooks with crawfish, goldfish (baby carp), or freshwater shrimp and cleaning the fish that could not resist those offerings. I often wondered if Bill Dance had ever endured such indignities.

On occasion, I also accompanied Mr. Strait when he visited his clients—the small restaurants and stores that bought his catfish. It was on one such day that his older friend joined us. I knew him as Mr. Frank. He was a thin, wiry, serious man, sort of like a banty rooster. He had an intimidating presence about him that left me feeling somewhat uncomfortable. Even though he was up in years, I could tell he was not a man with whom to trifle. He was friendly enough to me but in the don't-get-in-my-way-kid kind-of-way. The Delta was full of those old-school men.

IN THE PRESENCE OF HATRED

That day, we were all together at the Alamatt Moter Hotel in Greenville. The motel restaurant was a customer of Mr. Strait's. The Alamatt was one of those bygone motels that barely exist now. Nothing about it was attractive—it was all about function. It was basically a squared-up horseshoe with all rooms facing the swimming pool, fronted by the office and restaurant. I am sure it offered clean, plain rooms at an affordable price. We were just there to deliver catfish.

Mr. Strait had taken his business inside, leaving Mr.

Frank and me standing together and waiting for him to finish the transaction. As we casually stood there glancing around, we could not help but notice the lady swimming in the pool alone. To me, she stood out because on her head was a red rubber swimming cap, matching the color of her swimsuit. I remember thinking how odd that appeared (as in, who wore those anymore?) Shortly, she climbed out of the pool, approached the Coke machine, and attempted to purchase a soda. Nothing happened. No bottle emerged from the machine. She began to push buttons and shake the machine a bit.

There was someone else in that horseshoe that morning. He had been working quietly in a corner, painting the door of an empty room. He also witnessed the Coke machine distress of the woman. He stopped his painting to assist her. I took him to be an employee of the motel as he produced a key to the machine, opened it, gave her a soft drink, and returned to his painting. I saw someone lending a helping hand. Mr. Frank saw something entirely differently. The lady swimmer was white. The motel employee was black.

The intense hatred in his eyes still gets to me even now. It was chilling. It caught me completely off-guard in that moment. He was visibly shaking as he peered toward the black man; his hands clenched tightly into fists, veins in his neck popping out. Then he uttered the sentence that haunts me still. In a low but clear, hostile tone, he spoke: "Back in my day, we would lynch that N..." And I believed him.

Upon hearing this, initially, I became frightened— frightened for the black man, frightened for the woman, and frightened even for myself. I did not know what to expect. Was his wrath about to explode all over us? Next came confusion. Did I miss something? Had the black worker done or said something harmful to the woman? I took a minute or two to process Mr. Frank's reaction. I did not respond audibly to him. Truthfully, I did not know what to say. But finally, I understood. It was simply their interaction that evoked the rage. To Mr. Frank, a black man speaking publicly to a white woman—a swim-suited one at that—was anathema. It was unacceptable. It was a significant breach of the wall. It represented a total disruption of the proper order of life and was personally threatening to him. It was, in fact, something to potentially kill over.

Remarkably, I still feel a chill as I recount this story. It continues to impact me. Thankfully, it was the first and only one of the few times I witnessed pure, unfiltered hatred. It encapsulates for me an entire generation of people who were so blinded by racism that they could notice little else. Most folks in Greenville were not like Mr. Frank, but a few were. This watershed event in my life demonstrated what those Stein Mart protesters were striving to overcome.

KOSCIUSKO

Another came years later, while I was in college, in the small central Mississippi town of Kosciusko. Named after a Polish prince who fought to help America gain independence, it was also the town of my ancestors—the Whittington's. From here in Attala County, Ma Whit had moved to Greenville long before. It was a charming little town, different in many ways from Greenville. Life in Kosciusko revolved around its picturesque courthouse nestled in the middle of the downtown business district known as "the square." Several unexpected twists of life (more on that later) came together to deliver me to this town, but it became home for four college years.

During those years, I had the privilege of working for the small but successful Central Office Supply Company. It was a Kosciusko institution just off the square on a side street. The owner, Mr. Crowe, and his family treated me wonderfully. He allowed me to work around my class schedule, and the folks who worked there became like family. Many of us ate lunch together back in the printing department, which was a highlight of the working day. Not only was the food typically tasty, but we all drank the small eight-ounce Cokes, which the store kept in stock. An ongoing daily contest involving these drinks punctuated the lunch. A huge map was tacked to a wall. Back then the location of the bottling company was stamped onto the bottom of each Coke bottle. Whoever was unfortunate enough to have a bottle manufactured from the most distant town, as measured on that map, had to pay for everyone's soda. Frequent good-natured discussions erupted over how exact the measurements were, but it was all great fun. Working there was a delightful experience for me.

I did grunt work—cleaning up, a little shelf-stocking, furniture assembly—but mostly, I was the delivery boy. I learned every street, shortcut, and back alley of Kosciusko as I delivered copy paper and office supplies to nearly every business in town in the store's white panel van. I unexpectedly came face-to-face with the past during such a delivery to one of the town's venerated old drug stores on the square.

WHITE AND COLORED

The store pharmacist directed me to take the cases of

copy paper through some doors leading to a back supply room. As I guided my dolly past the old-fashioned soda fountain, past shelves of aspirin and other medications, and toward the doors, I was sure I was only thinking about getting this job done to move on to the next. I most definitely was not expecting to have such a life-impacting encounter, but I did.

For some, this may not seem like that kind of impactful moment. As I recall it now, I sometimes wonder why it affected me. It was simply a leftover relic from the past—even then. Nothing but some faded words over doors, but I had never personally seen this before, even in Greenville. Two doors were on the opposite wall as I walked into the storeroom. Above one was the words, "Whites Only." Above the other was painted just one word, "Colored." I am not exactly sure how long I stood there taking this in. I finally figured out that, at one time, this was likely a doctor's office with two doors segregating the patients. At this point in my life, I was well aware of Mississippi's track record of segregation; I had seen photographs of similar scenes, but here I was standing in one—now a remnant of history, but still very real. Emotions overwhelmed me, thinking, so this is how it must have felt to live on the other side of the wall. The indignity of it all, of being treated lesser, of being socialized out of the mainstream through a side door. In that room, in that moment, somehow, some way, I felt as if I experienced it all.

Don't misunderstand. I was not some social warrior politically engaged in working against racial injustice. I was a product of my environment—a boy from Greenville, Mississippi, still trying to sort many things out. But the surprise waiting for me in the drug store storeroom deeply moved me. Was it bringing together all my previous experiences? Was it because my college roommate was black? I still cannot thoroughly explain it, but the words and what they represented burned deeply into my heart. My mind went back to that day at Stein Mart. Undoubtedly, most of those singing and carrying those signs were made to file through doors with "Colored" written above them. Well, I thought, at least, they had overcome that.

The experience in that room made me appreciate the courage demonstrated on that day in Greenville in an entirely different way. I never hear that song anywhere anymore except in the recesses of my mind. I believe it is still an appropriate refrain as we continue to work out the complexities of racial struggles.

"We shall overcome someday." Yes, I pray, perhaps someday, we will.

MEMORIES AND MORE:

- Since my Greenville days, I have frequented other Stein Marts in different locations. Sadly, the one in my current city in Arkansas closed. While I found bargains, none could compare with Greenville's first and original store. It was a special place with clothes and goods piled everywhere. (I don't think much thought was given to product presentation then). The Charley Conerly Shoe Store was connected to it, which was named after a former Ole Miss (the University of Mississippi in Oxford) football great. My sister, Donna, worked there as a teen. Stein Mart represented the Greenville melting pot, as everyone, regardless of race, came there to shop. The Steins were excellent merchants. They had another store not far away on Broadway. "Sam Stein's" sold upper-scale clothing at higher prices. Only very occasionally did I get to shop there.

- Believe it or not, back then, kids were allowed to walk or bike down city sidewalks and roam around neighborhoods without adult supervision. When we went out to play, we were just told to be back by supper. It was delightful.

- The depression. I did not have to live through that problematic era in American history, but it helped form me through my grandmother, Ma Whit. Looking back, it seemed she continued to live it; saving, conserving, and repurposing everything was her nature. If she ever found herself eating out at a restaurant (a rare treat then), she would snatch up the packets of sugar, ketchup, and jelly left on the table to use later at home. She hardly threw away any leftover food. They would end up in her to-die-for soup or some other dish. She was a seamstress, and every inch of fabric was precious. She wasted very little. Her need for thrift still lingers within me.

- Dr. Martin Luther King, Jr., remains a seminal figure in American history. There is not much I can say to add to his legacy and impact. Yet, it seems to me that some of that has been forgotten or reimagined. What continues to impress me is his nonviolent approach, humility, and courage. He sledgehammered that invisible wall with eloquent tenacity but never sought to harm anyone. His death was a true loss for all. He is a real American hero.

- If you ever want to learn about the Civil Rights movement in Mississippi and perhaps experience some of the emotions of that turbulent time, visit the Mississippi Civil Rights Museum in Jackson, Mississippi. It faithfully chronicles the struggle, has engaging displays and artifacts, and preserves both the tragedies and triumphs of this history.

4

Not Separate But Not Together Either

Rapid changes came to my world in Greenville. I left Broadway behind both by graduating from Ella Darling and by moving to another part of town. Arnold Avenue became my new address, and Solomon Junior High became my new school.

Solomon was not a "middle school." We knew no such terminology then. It housed grades seven through nine and was named, like Ella Darling, after a legendary Greenville educator. At Solomon, my world expanded. Ray, Stanley, Orange, and Frog were all left back on Broadway. Eddie, Wesley, Buddy, Harvey, and Kevin became my crew throughout high school. Kids from all over Greenville were shuttled into Solomon---by parents, bicycles, and buses. We got to experience the new challenge of changing classes each period instead of remaining in the same classroom all day. We tried out for the school sports teams. It was all new and cool, but it also created a level of anxiety. In Junior High fashion, we all desperately wanted to fit in—to be accepted. That included the black kids, too, of course.

Solomon was in a white section of town. The brand-new concept of a shopping mall was being built directly across from the school. No black students lived nearby. It was not their side of the wall. I never really paused to consider the additional challenges they faced. I was too busy worrying about my own insecurities. How things fell in place then at Solomon between black and white represented how life would be the rest of the way through school. It consisted of a common acceptance of the situation, a cordial getting-along with each other that on occasion created friendships, playing sports together and in class together, doing science lab together, etc., but with some rare exceptions, nothing too meaningful beyond that. In all of our hunting and fishing trips, crazy misadventures to come, and friendly shenanigans, my crew never invited anyone of color to join us. Nor did we receive any such invitations from our black classmates. We were not totally separate, but not totally together either. This became the rhythm of life interrupted by only the occasional disturbance.

HONKY

One such disturbance for me developed quickly after arriving at Solomon. It brought with it a new word into my vocabulary. For reasons known only to him, an older black student targeted me to shake down each day for lunch milk money. Maybe as a scrawny, skinny kid, I looked like an easy mark. He used bully tactics like threatening and intimidating me for a quarter. This was an unwelcome new experience for me. At first, I was, as we used to say, "scared to death" and meekly handed over the money. After only a few days of this—missing my milk at lunch—I somehow realized it had to end. So, I mustered up enough courage to eventually say "no" to him, threatening him back in the only way I thought might work— ratting him out to a teacher. He tried calling my bluff, but I was determined and refused to hand over the quarter. To my great surprise and delight, I did not get clobbered, and he left me alone after that. But I did learn that new word.

Initially, I thought he called me a "donkey." Not that this would have been a new zinger, but it would have been an unusual one. Instead, I finally understood it more clearly. He called me a "honky." Honestly, I had no idea what that meant—only later discovering it was a kind of counter to the N-word white folks used. It soon spread and was frequently heard on campus, but it never stung. There was nothing behind it—no history or hurt. It became a joke of sorts to us, and white kids began calling each other honky.

THE COACH

Solomon had an integrated teaching and administrative staff. One of the most feared among them was Coach Cartilige. He had once been a coach somewhere, but at Solomon, he was a vice-principal. He was a large man, no doubt once a dominant athlete, and he still gave off the vibe that he could hold his own in any sport. He seemed to always carry a paddle with him. He had the reputation of blistering the bottoms of any unruly kid (nothing scandalous about that then). And he was black. Everything I just mentioned for my crew influenced us to give Coach Cartilige a wide birth and do all we could to stay on his good side, except maybe the last thing I noted. He could have been green—we just wanted no part of his paddle.

But I came ever so close to it. During my last year at Solomon, we were required to take a language course. I had zero interest but chose Spanish. Apparently, few others in the class were interested in it either. It became rowdy fairly quickly. The unfortunate teacher, a young guy, was fresh off the teaching farm and was ultimately in over his head. He had a perpetual bewilderedness about him. We smelled blood and pounced. He had great difficulty controlling us; consequently, we learned very little. Of course, the administration knew this. Trips to the office were frequent from his class. Somehow, I had avoided that dubious honor until one fateful morning.

Things were chaotic as usual. The teacher was futilely trying to corral us. I do not recall what he was attempting to say, but I do remember yelling above the noise, "You tell 'em about it, Mr. Lang!" Have you ever heard the story about the principal listening to the class over a two-way speaker? I thought that was pure myth. Trust me, it is not. As soon as those words escaped my lips, the booming voice of Coach Cartilige descended upon us as if God himself were present—out of that speaker. "Please immediately send the young man who spoke those words to my office. I have a few things to tell him," he commanded. An indescribable fog of fear settled over me.

Impending doom awaited. The walk to that office on rubber legs has to be one of the longest of my life. Coach Cartilige! The paddle! I began hyperventilating. I was a dead man walking for sure. But it was not to be. Surprisingly, Coach Cartilige did not take me to the woodshed, even though he could have. Instead, he laid on me one of the most extensive guilt trips ever presented over our treatment of the Spanish teacher. In retrospect, it was a brilliant maneuver. After all, I certainly did not want to be responsible for ruining the life and career of this new teacher. Before it was over, Coach Cartilige had me partner with him to salvage Mr. Lang's job. I apologized and did everything I could to message sorrow—anything to avoid that paddle's swift, painful justice. From then on, I gave the Spanish teacher a break. From then on, there was no man I respected more at Solomon Junior High School than Coach Cartilige. He reminded me of a lesson I had learned years before with ole Mose: that proper respect is not earned through fear. It is gained through the character of a person.

HIGH SCHOOL

Solomon gave way to T. L. Weston, formerly Greenville's black high school but now hosting only tenth graders. Even then, I thought having a school just for sophomores was a convoluted situation. It was the opposite of Solomon in that it was in a black neighborhood, and white kids came from a distance to attend. I don't recall anyone liking it, but not because of where it was. We were supposed to be in high school, but we were separated from the main campus and isolated. I don't believe this setup lasted very long after our class. Of course, it was that way as Greenville public schools struggled with a growing student population while attempting to balance integration fairly.

Finally, we reached Greenville High School, home of the mighty Hornets. One Hornet who made it to the NFL, Wilbert Montgomery, was a star running back for the Philadelphia Eagles in my high school years. We all were proud. Sports have a way of transcending race.

Life at GHS was much like it had been before. There were some white teachers and some black teachers. The student population in my class was probably about evenly represented—half white, half black. We had few problems. We hung out at school but still did not hang out much anywhere else. I did develop a close school friendship with one black student, Jesse.

LIBRARY DUTY

Being somewhat of a slacker, I had no desire to join any school club, but we were required to do so. Thinking I could skate through reasonably easily, I joined the library club. Boy, was I wrong. Much to my chagrin, I had to be a library monitor, which involved hanging out there more often than I ever desired. Jesse made it easier, though. He was there for more noble reasons—he enjoyed books. Tall and athletic, Jesse was the complete opposite of the library nerd stereotype. Over time and books, Jesse and I grew close. I came to admire Jesse's dedication to scholarship, something we did not share. We happily exchanged our life experiences with each other. We talked about school and interests; we talked about home, but we never actually went to each other's house. Not once did our friendship extend beyond the walls of GHS. I don't think it ever occurred to me to pursue that—I'm not sure about him. There was no ill intent to this. It's just the way it was. We were not separate, but we were still not together—that invisible but very real wall continued to exist. We had not yet overcome.

One frequent topic of conversation between Jesse and me was girls. He was somewhat more accomplished than me in this department. Almost all the other guys were. Eddie and Wesley had girlfriends in my crew, with the latter fashioning himself with what we would now call "a player." Me, not so much. I was too shy and awkward. That was, until the last semester of my senior year. Finally, as I was about to exit high school life, I found puppy love, or rather, it found me.

The memory remains crystal clear—walking down the hall to English class with a buddy, he noticed this pretty girl looking my way. He nudged me. I glanced over, and our eyes met. I did not know her—she was in the junior class. I moved on, not thinking much more about it, and the memory would likely be lost entirely to me, except for what happened the next day. Walking down that hall again, I am suddenly in a big collision. Books fly everywhere! It is that girl. I ran smack into her. I apologize, ask if she is okay, help retrieve her books, and head on into class. Then, believe it or not—the same scenario played out the following day.

My first reaction was to wonder if this girl needed glasses (yes, I was every bit that dense). It wasn't until a couple of days later that I got it, but only after one of her girlfriends, with whom I attended art class, clued me to the fact that Sandra thought I was cute and would be interested in possibly going out with me. I realize how dated this story sounds, but back then, proper girls did not call boys or ask them out. That was considered too forward. No cell phones existed to Snapchat anyone, so they had to resort to efforts like this to get our attention and penetrate our thick skulls. She was a lovely girl. I was amazed that this pretty, brown-haired, blue-eyed girl was interested in me. We enjoyed several fun dates, including going to dances together.

I always enjoyed dancing and attended a few off-campus school dances. As my senior year neared its conclusion, plans were afoot for a big senior dance downtown, off Washington Avenue, in what I knew as the "teen club." Plans were made to go, but as I shared this news with Jesse, he had received no such invitation. As I soon discovered, few of the other black students had either. I was aware that since desegregation, there no longer existed such things as official school dances, school senior trips, or any other large school-sponsored social gatherings—all of which my older sisters had enjoyed. I had just assumed it was due to our sheer numbers. My graduating class had over 500 students; the other classes boasted similar numbers. Perhaps that was part of it, but looking back, I believe other factors were also in play—that invisible wall that continued to separate us. So, on a late May evening, we all gathered on the football field, celebrated our class accomplishments, joyfully received our diplomas, threw our caps into the air, and then went our separate ways. Sandra and I, along with other white students, danced the night away. I never saw Jesse again. Life moved on. Most moved on with it, but the Delta stayed the same in some ways.

MOREHEAD

I was in transition for sure. As college neared, I had no real direction or ambition—just floating along, waiting for something to happen. This led me directly to Mississippi Delta Junior College in nearby Morehead, Mississippi. Absolutely nothing was wrong with this community college, forever affectionately known simply as "Morehead" (The beloved cheer of "Go-head Mo-head" was commonly heard.). Still, it was nothing to get excited about for me, especially since I commuted there each day with other day students on an old bus.

I made a few new friends while at Morehead—some guys like me were more driven to hang out at the student center playing foosball, ping pong, and mostly cards— mostly the game of Spades. Along with new friends, Bill, Kemp, and a few others, we dedicated ourselves to this game and bonded over it. We partnered with and played against each other. Bill and I, though, gelled into an almost unbeatable combination. In all transparency, we were not above bending the rules a bit. We developed a code to inform one another if we had a dominant suit in our hand. If we were heavy with hearts, we would "innocently" mention something about indigestion or heartburn or rub our chest. If diamonds dominated, a ring, earring, or other jewelry would suddenly become part of the conversation. Feet, shoes, walking, or a painful toe would represent clubs (also known as "puppy feet"). If we were heavy with spades, that is when we would mention Kemp --because he was black. At that moment, it never occurred to us how insensitive and insulting this was. "Spades" was another of those unfortunate terms used in a negative way to describe black people. To me even at this point, it was not on the same level as that word, so I decided it was okay to use. We certainly meant no harm. Kemp seemed cool with it, laughing it off and never indicating offense. Bill and I thought it to be nothing but a lark. Looking back, there was little chance that Kemp shared that feeling. It had to hurt him, but we just ignorantly played on, not once considering the consequences of our words.

All these years later, I've wondered if that worked to prevent a closer relationship with Kemp during that Morehead year. Bill and I planned a camping and fishing trip on Lake Lee near Greenville in the spring semester. Kemp had often shared his love for fishing, but try as we did, he would not accompany us. Hanging out in the student center was one thing, but outside of it—well, that invisible wall we were contributing to stood tall and was not made any less real by our actions. Not separate, but still not together.

Truthfully, during that year, I had no real drive and goofed around as a commuter student, working part-time at the Kroger grocery store in Greenville. It did not help that most of my high school crew—for various unexpected reasons—stayed close to home that year, too. We all continued to hang out, trying to figure out what was next and our place in life. That became clear during yet another steamy Delta summer after those wasted semesters at Morehead.

Through my friend Eddie's father, I got a job at a small company that made parts for the grain bins that stood everywhere on Delta farms. I worked on the shipping dock. It was often hot and hard work, but now, I would not trade anything in the world for it. It was there I met a man named Hoss. It was during this summer that I met my

Lord for the first time, and suddenly, everything changed in ways I could not have anticipated in my wildest dreams.

MEMORIES AND MORE:

- Greenville was an amazing city in its day. The number of gifted people from the city in the literary field over the years is impressive. A few professional athletes also have Greenville roots. The Carter family produced several famous folks. All came from this small city of around 50,000 people at its zenith. But things have changed for the Queen City. The loss of population and industry has made Greenville a shell of my growing-up days. A drive through the city now reveals crumbling infrastructure, empty buildings, and faded glory. The poverty level remains relatively high, but a dedicated population remains, and they are working diligently to revitalize the city. I hope they succeed. If you ever desire to learn more about Greenville and the Mississippi Delta—the culture, the embedded historical and social forces at play, the consequences of the invisible wall, and perhaps why it has fallen upon more challenging times, I recommend reading *The Most Southern Place on the Earth: The Mississippi Delta and The Roots of Regional Identity* by James C. Cobb. It is a bit dated now, but it offers a fascinating glimpse into the history of Greenville and the Delta and why the town and region have diminished.

- Malls were coming to Greenville! This was beyond exciting news to us kids. It was a new-to-Greenville concept—inside shopping! It's hard to believe how pumped we were about that, but both of them, especially the Greenville Mall near Solomon, became a regular hang-out. A large chunk of the meager money we managed to scrape up went into the pinball and game machines at Odd Oz, which was the arcade in the mall. This mall still stands but is also diminished with fewer stores and a past-its-prime feel. But in its day, it was the destination location for many a Delta kid.

- The word "honky" as an insult never gained much ground in my youth. We got that it was an attempt to counter the N-word, to clap back at the pain that word caused. But there was no emotional baggage with it, no cruel history to prop it up and give it weight. So, we just laughed it off on our side of the wall. Toward those on the other side, it was not just the N-word but an entire lexicon of damaging slang that was used. Just my ignorant usage of the word "spade" illustrates that. That was a joke to me. It meant nothing, but I failed to realize it was just as demeaning as that other word I put aside years before. Words matter. Even now. If we could learn to use them to build up one another instead of tearing each other down.

- One privilege we eagerly anticipated as we moved into Weston during our sophomore year was the ability to leave campus during lunch. Never before had we had this opportunity. It came with that even more anticipated milestone

—being old enough for a driver's license (not that this mattered to most of us since getting our own car was a pipe dream at this point). But a few fortunate folks did have their own cars, and, equally excitingly, the first ever McDonald's in Greenville opened up just as school began. Wow. This was all the buzz. We could not wait. So, as this perfect storm of events converged, we found ourselves crammed into someone's car, dashing across town to score a Big Mac while having to make it back to Weston, all in 30 minutes. Yep, that was all the time we were allotted to exercise our newfound lunch freedom. As you might guess, that was not a sustainable situation. The school lunchroom once more seemed to be just fine. Even today, the buttered rolls they served are legendary.

- Guys, today, have it easy. In the mid-70s, we had to do all of the work. Girls were prohibited from initiating overt contact with boys regarding romance or dating. Guys had to call and officially invite the girl out. We had to go to their homes, meet her parents, spend time answering questions, pay for everything, and ensure we had them home by curfew. To call this intimidating is an understatement. All things considered, it is incredible that what was then still called "courtship" even happened. But love, yes, even puppy love, always finds a way.

5

Hoss And Conversion

"Go see Hoss!" I was instructed on my first day of work at the Reed-Joseph Company. Reed-Joseph was one of those small businesses that, at one point in history, helped serve as the economic foundation of cities like Greenville. It was flourishing then, employing dozens of people from skilled to unskilled labor—making and shipping every single part of a grain bin. I was among the unskilled laborers, working a summer job on the shipping dock, sorting and loading all that sheet metal onto trucks of all sizes. The heat and humidity of the Delta bouncing off the metal often gave me the sensation of working in a furnace. It was sweaty work with long hours, but I was happy to have the job.

Hoss was the "tool man"—the guy who checked out all of the assorted tools to any who needed them in the company. He worked in the tool cage, of course. Anyone who needed a tool knew Hoss. So off I was sent to him on my first day to retrieve what I was told was an essential tool for the project—a bolt stretcher. I made haste to get there, moving around forklifts, piles of sheet metal, cutting machines, and anyone in my way to get the tool as fast as possible. After all, I wanted to make a good impression that first day.

At first glance, Hoss was not an impressive-looking guy. He was of average build, with short, cropped, graying hair and deep wrinkles lining his face. His eyes were a light brown. His skin was a shade of hazelnut. He was quick with a smile and always seemed to have a twinkle in his eyes. In one sense, he seemed really old, but his body defied his age when he moved. He was a calm presence in the deadline pressure the job often created. He always spoke softly and deliberately. He was an institution all unto himself at Reed-Joseph. As I came to find out, Hoss had earned the respect of all the workers.

BOLT STRETCHER

At that moment, however, I could only think about the bolt stretcher. As I made this request to Hoss, a brief smile spread over his face, and a little chuckle escaped his lips. While I did not know what was up, he did. He replied, "You are new here, aren't you, son?" Of course, I was, but now was no time for small talk. In my mind, the fate of an entire project waited on the bolt stretcher! He recognized my apparent eagerness along with my naiveté and tried to ease my anxiety. He explained that what I sought did not exist; instead, it was a long-standing, common prank. My being sent off in a rush to him was a good-hearted joke by the guys on the shipping dock. Hoss explained that it was an initiation, a trick played on all newbies. It occurred to me that all those guys were having a big laugh at my adventure. I am sure Hoss saw my crestfallen look, but he assured me it was all good. To play along, he produced an impressive-looking instrument for me to take back. "Tell 'em you got their bolt stretcher," he laughed. We all ended up hee-hawing over the episode. This was my memorable first encounter with Hoss.

I slowly learned all my responsibilities on the shipping dock over that summer. I especially enjoyed the opportunities to drive the forklift or, even better, operate the crane. The crane was mounted on tracks overhead. It picked up massive amounts of metal, moved that weight along its tracks, and deposited it on the big flatbed trucks that more-than-often filled up the shipping dock. For an eighteen-year-old guy, this wasn't necessarily work; it was fun. Unfortunately, the forklift and crane work only happened infrequently for me as the "low-guy-on-the-totem-pole." More often, I was manhandling the smaller parts stacked outside in that sauna-like Delta air. As a result, the lunch break became the most anticipated part of the day. It offered the opportunity to escape the heat, rest momentarily, and enjoy whatever deliciousness was in my lunchbox.

FIRST STEPS TO FAITH

Back to my roots on South Broadway, I lived with my grandmother that summer. It was a move I needed to make, and Ma Whit gladly welcomed me. I had purchased my first car—a brown 1966 Volkswagen Beetle with a standard transmission, which meant I got to shift the gears manually. That was treacherous at first but fun later. As a result, I was enjoying an even greater sense of independence than the year at Morehead offered. Ma Whit did her best to spoil me in good, grandmotherly fashion. Her lunches were always impressive, even if they were just sandwiches. Lunch became the center around which the rest of the day was built at Reed-Joseph.

Lunch also allowed me to become better acquainted with Hoss. There was a spot designated as a break area. It was located near the tool cage, but few took advantage of it. Most preferred to eat with their long-time work buddies. Not having such, I gravitated to the spot. Hoss was there and welcomed the company. At first, it felt somewhat awkward due to the age difference, but there were also other noticeable differences that were quickly overcome. Hoss and I began to share life over a sandwich, a Zero candy bar, and a Barq's Root Beer.

Hoss, I learned, was a widower, having lost his wife a few years prior. He had children, but they were all adults with their own children. Hoss was happy that they all remained around Greenville. Slowly, I learned how he was an institution at Reed-Joseph—employed there for more years, it seemed, than he could count. He was a virtual, walking, and talking encyclopedia regarding tools. Looking back, I am not sure if that company could have operated without him. He was a humble, non-assuming man with a kind and compassionate manner. Despite our differences, we became friends.

Our lunch conversations covered various topics, from sports to fishing to cars to company news to religion. I quickly discovered that Hoss was a profoundly religious man, and God seemed to be central to all of his conversations. He even prayed before we dug into our lunch offerings—for me, a practice reserved only for a big Thanksgiving meal. I was never sure which church Hoss attended, but there was little doubt that it was some charismatic church, what old-timers in the Mississippi Delta called the "holy rollers." I just knew enough about them to recognize them, I suppose. As a teen, one of my uncles delighted in spinning a yarn about participating in a "holy roller" revival. There, as he told it, "looking for a girl but finding only the Holy Ghost." Of course, this terminology was unflattering and unkind, but again, it was the language of that time and place, which fortunately—for the most part—remains there.

Religion in my family came from my paternal grandfather. He was a dedicated "Campbellite" (a now obscure term referencing a pioneer preacher, Alexander Campbell, who was influential in shaping and forming the Churches of Christ. It was used by some then in an unflattering way to describe folks in Churches of Christ.) Grandaddy had been a carpenter, itinerant farmer, and a shipyard worker, among other things, but through it all, a stalwart Christian —a song leader and faithful to Churches of Christ. Not all of his sons shared that same level of commitment.

As a consequence, neither did some of their children (one of the exceptions was my oldest sister, Donna. Her faith would become an essential part of my story). As a kid, I attended the South Main Church of Christ in Greenville occasionally. Vacation Bible School was, for a time, a highlight of the summer (they served cookies and juice!). Gradually, my family drifted away. Church was not much of a part of my life except for Christmas and Easter. But enough had sunk in somehow for me to recognize, although fuzzy, that I could not buy all that Hoss was selling in our conversations.

READING THE BIBLE

As our discussions about God, religion, and church grew more profound, I realized that I could not go along with all of the charismatic leanings expressed by Hoss. Churches of Christ were quite different, and I remember trying to explain it to him—like I knew a great deal about it. I found myself on unequal footing as he shared his beliefs, quoted the Bible, and explained what it meant. Looking to shore up my feeble knowledge, I turned to the Bible, really reading it for the first time in my life. Yet, I was at a loss. I had no idea where to turn (both figuratively and literally). Ma Whit was certainly a believer but would be what we now call "unchurched." While she did try to help, I discovered she was not the best resource. I turned to my grandfather, but he ended up preaching a sermon to me more than anything else. Next, I asked my sister, Donna, who provided me the kind of help I needed—Bible verses to counter Hoss's Bible verses. I was just "in it to win it" and to prove that my take on things was correct. So, I went to Hoss with all this accumulated ammunition. It was, as my dad once described it, mental gymnastics and, as I now realize, not a healthy way to approach the Bible.

Several wonderful, amazing, and unexpected developments happened during this process, not the least of which came from Hoss himself. Instead of digging in and taking my argumentative approach, he listened to what I shared. He took it all in in his quiet way. This is one reason why his memory stands out to me now. He could have responded by shutting me down, by taming the young, know-it-all white boy, but he did not. The result was that we began studying the Bible and praying together over those lunch breaks. No way, no how, at any time previous to this would this scenario have been imagined.

My seeking aid from Donna, who lived in Cleveland, Mississippi (another nearby Delta town that is home to Delta State University) at the time, eventually led to her bringing a young man who was serving as a summer intern in the youth program at her church to visit me at Ma Whit's house. When first mentioned, I did not welcome this. Speaking to someone so close to my age made me nervous—after all, in all of my huff and puff, I knew very little about the Bible. Mike was a nice, likable guy. He invited me to come over to Cleveland to hang out with him and the college kids at home there that summer. I was willing to give that a shot and found it surprisingly fun. The church had a student center on the university's campus, which was practically empty during the summer. The youth group had full access to it, including a ping pong table. Quickly, my weekends included a trip to Donna's house, playing marathon ping pong, and gradually even staying over for church on Sunday. This was a most unexpected development for me, but it impacted me. That was for sure.

A TRUE LIFE CHANGE

After a while, my big topic became baptism—something I had never done. Baptism in Churches of Christ is a fundamental teaching I discovered in numerous New Testament texts on its purpose and significance as an expression of faith in Christ. Mike urged me to be baptized. Donna urged me to be baptized. My grand-daddy, I knew without even asking, would be all in since he mentioned it to me almost every occasion I visited him. But I also wanted to know what Hoss thought. After all, I felt that those talks over lunch with him started me on this journey—even if my initial part of it was wrongheaded. Hoss was thrilled to hear about it. He may have had a different church background, but he was all in for me, "finding the Lord." He joined the chorus of those urging me to do it, though only if I meant it in my heart.

So I did! Late one Saturday night in the baptistry of the Church of Christ in Cleveland, I was immersed into Jesus Christ and my life changed forever. In biblical terms, I became a "new creation," having all my sins washed away in the blood of Christ. Not knowing much of the theology then, I just felt renewed—like God had given me a fresh start, a chance to do something different, maybe something that mattered with my life. It started even that night. Less than one hour after being baptized, I found myself, along with Mike and other teens, witnessing to young people who had gathered in a parking lot to hang out. I recall telling my story to a couple of guys sitting in a car—the smoke and smell of weed emerging from the vehicle as they lowered their window. They listened to my story and then happily replied how cool it was that I was high on Jesus! It was cool. I felt it and wanted the rest of the world to feel it, too.

That included Hoss. I came back to work all fired up. Hoss rejoiced in the news of my baptism and patiently put up with my attempt to convert him to all things involving

Churches of Christ doctrine. Lunch became about this now. I immediately wanted to know about his baptism, if he had been baptized, and began throwing at him the few Bible verses I knew. As was his custom, he calmly took it all in.

It also included Ma Whit. I returned to her house, determined that I should also convince her to be baptized. Even more than Hoss, I "pounded" at her with my passion to convert the world. Looking back, I had to have been obnoxious and unrelenting, which the Bible calls "zeal without knowledge." At that point, I did not know what I did not know. But what I did know, I thought everyone else should know as well, so I kept at them. It was a wonderful new existence for me, but maybe not so much for others in my life!

CHURCH WALLS

Yet everything in it was not always wonderful. I soon discovered (never having a reason to recognize this before) that segregation still existed in churches. That invisible wall was present among the faithful, too. In Greenville, this meant that the church-of-my-growing-up-years was populated by white folks only (It was not that the South Main church was racist. Segregation in churches was just the way it had always been in my lifetime, and as far as I know, no one from either of these black or white churches was pushing to change that). The black people attended the Highway 82 Church of Christ (Our church is not very imaginative when naming our congregations—typically, we go with the street it is located on.) As I settled into a routine of attending worship and becoming involved in the youth activities at the South Main congregation, I began asking about that other church in town. I discovered that little was known about them, which did not sit right. I then became determined to change that, and one day, the perfect opportunity presented itself. It was called a "gospel meeting." This is the Church of Christ's term for a revival. The Highway 82 church was putting one on with its brand-new preacher.

From the moment I returned from Cleveland after my conversion, I started putting pressure on both Hoss and my grandmother not only to be baptized but also to attend church with me. Initially, both efforts failed. Hoss deferred, stating that the white folks in my church would not accept him (I countered that they would, and besides, who cared if they didn't?). Being in her upper 70s, Ma Whit replied that it would be difficult health-wise. I kept on nagging them, however. Now that I found the Lord, I desperately wanted everyone else to, especially those I cared about. Nothing was going to stand in my way either. I was that determined to convert the world. I could not understand why anyone would not want the new-found joy I had discovered. And I was just getting started! I received more fuel for my fire in an unexpected place.

A NEW EXPERIENCE

Brother Loyd Harris was the young, new, dynamic evangelist for the Highway 82 Church. (As it happens, Loyd and I currently work in the same city.) The small church building was solidly packed—hardly any pew space was available. The air conditioners were straining to ease the late summer haze of heat surrounding us outside. Several had little hand fans to aid in stirring up the breeze. Everyone was dressed immaculately. The atmosphere was electric with a sense of anticipation—an expectation that God was working there. As I gazed around the big room, it was not hard to notice that I was the only white person. I was greeted warmly and made to feel at home, even if I noticed a few what-is-that-white-boy-doing-here looks. The singing was energizing and quite different than what I had experienced. The church was vocal, with both men and women occasionally raising an amen or hallelujah. It fired me up. Then, brother Harris took to the pulpit. His preaching style was powerful and poetic. He held sway with the audience, offering their full support. I sat immersed in his message—an hour passed without noticing. Wow. I was ready for more.

More came from what was commonly referred to within Churches of Christ as a "door-knocking campaign." It was all new to me then, but it meant folks went door-to-door in neighborhoods, inviting people to church, revival, and Bible study. The Highway 82 Church was going to conduct one that Saturday to support their new preacher's revival efforts. I decided to join in. Loyd eagerly encouraged me, so on that Saturday, I knocked on doors along Clay Street—the same street we used to walk through to get to the swimming pool. Again, I was so into this that I was unaware of the racial optics here. The folks answering the doors may have thought seeing me on the other side strange, but all acted cordially.

During this time, I continued to badger both Hoss and my grandmother, thinking that since Hoss helped me begin this journey and Ma Whit, well, she was my grandmother with whom I lived, and both needed the blessings I had discovered. I had related in glowing terms to Hoss about the glorious time I was enjoying at the Highway 82 church —compelling him to attend. I put it in life-or-death terms. Eternity was on the line! As was his manner, Hoss just absorbed it all and went on about his business. I became frustrated that my efforts were failing, but little did I know.

After the door-knocking efforts, it was the Saturday night of that revival. It appeared that those efforts generated some results as guests were arriving. It was another warm night. I was about to head inside to find cooler air when I noticed him. Making his way across the busy highway was Hoss! I could hardly believe my eyes. I ran over to him. He said, "I had to see what all the commotion was about." He had walked from his home, which, as it turned out, was fairly nearby. I am not sure why his arrival affected me so. Seeing him—this man who had befriended me, taught me, listened to me, put up with me—walking across that highway moved me. Throughout that summer, I had basically "trashed" many of his religious views, slammed his church affiliation, and bothered him relentlessly about baptism and church attendance. Again, at that stage, my passion got the best of me. I had much to learn about the grace of God. But still, here was Hoss.

Even now, as I recall this night, it carries with it a twinge in my heart. I was elated! Hoss enjoyed the entire experience so much that he occasionally visited the Highway 82 congregation. One regret I have is that I do not know what happened to Hoss. Shortly after, life got hectic as I prepared to move to that college in Kosciusko. My job ended, and I lost touch with Hoss, but I will never forget this kind, gentle man. He certainly was a steady, guiding force for me during this part of my life—patiently putting up with my uninformed exuberance while at the same time not attempting to damper my fledgling faith. He was just the right person at the right time for me, but that was no accident. I did not—perhaps could not—comprehend it at the time, but I now believe that he was one of many grace-filled souls that God has put in my path to guide and teach me better his will and way.

AN UNFORGETTABLE EVENT

Just as Hoss had heard more than I imagined he had, so did my grandmother. She, too, bore the brunt of my zeal with great long-suffering. I was unrelenting, becoming like my paternal grandfather in preaching to her. In retrospect, it is a wonder that she did not boot me out of her house. I was that persistent and, well, rude. However, God's grace managed to squeeze through despite me somewhere in all of that pounding. On a Wednesday night in the late summer of 1977, I was sitting mid-way back in the sanctuary of the South Main Church of Christ in Greenville, MS. I witnessed the incredible, unimaginable, beautiful image of the love and mercy of God.

The South Main church building was a product of its time and place. Later, as I began visiting Churches of Christ throughout Mississippi and the South, it became apparent that many congregations used the same architectural firm. Like South Main, they featured long auditoriums with a single aisle in the middle, with high-pitched ceilings adorned with polished wood support beams visible from the inside. Then, green seemed to have been the overwhelming choice of carpet color. I decided there was a certain inviting and comforting charm about it all.

Of course, one of the most expected features was what was absent in any Church of Christ. That would be a piano or organ. Churches of Christ were famously (or infamously, according to whom you were speaking) instrument-free. Most remain so. It was part of our identity, based solidly on our interpretation of certain Bible verses. The term for that is *a cappela*, which originally meant "in the manner of the chapel." Now, it refers to singing without musical accompaniment.

Larry Roberts was the preacher for the South Main

church during this time. While Loyd Harris was all fury and eloquence, Larry, while able to work up a lather himself as he preached, was generally more subdued. Most of all, though, he was an encourager—an extremely cheerful man I enjoyed being around. His son, Robby, had been in my class at Greenville High. He was highly regarded among his peers, having been elected class president. Both father and son welcomed me to the flock.

Larry's voice announced it to the assembled: Two people had requested baptism that night, and preparations were about to be made. Before that, there would be the confession of faith in Christ. First up, he announced, was Vallie Whittington! The feeling and impact of that moment still return when I allow myself to recall it. I sat stunned, thinking perhaps I had misheard and then experiencing pure, humbling joy. My grandmother, that grand old lady with whom I had harassed, was standing there in front of the church, confessing Christ, about to put him on in baptism. I will admit to tears flowing. It was surreal. Despite my bumbling efforts, God's grace had penetrated her heart. It remains one of the most amazing moments of my life. Incredible. After so many years lived, she was not above humbling herself, submitting her will to the Father and being born again of the water and the Spirit. Amazing.

With that wonderful occasion, Ma Whit also became part of the South Main church—although I am not sure she ever ultimately bought into every aspect of the Church of Christ. I only had a few more weeks in her home after that. Through the urging of Larry Roberts, I decided to attend a brand-new Bible college in the Beehive of the Hills, Kosciusko. It was all new and exciting to me. After coming to Christ and being fired up about my conversion, it only made sense that I would move toward full-time ministry. Ma Whit was happy for me and happy I was returning to the town of her birth. With this, my life continued to change and grow in directions unimagined just a few months before.

That became the pivotal summer of my life—a redefining of myself and my purpose in life. This time, I left Greenville properly behind me, never to return permanently. Yet, Greenville always remains with me—all my experiences at the levee, along Broadway, Washington Avenue, and Clay Street, between meeting Ole Mose and Hoss. With this move, the invisible wall that remained erected in Greenville, separating Jesse and me, separating the churches, and dividing the races, came crashing down —at least in my life. I was about to enter a whole new world.

MEMORIES AND MORE:

- Hoss does represent how God brings different people into our lives at various times. Often, these people are from other backgrounds— almost like God is forcing us to adjust, rethink, and broaden our minds. He calls us to be "new wineskins" (Matthew 9:17). In Biblical times wineskins were containers made out of animal skin to hold and store new wine. It was imperative not to use an old wineskin for new wine since the old skin had lost its ability to flex and be shaped by the new, fermenting wine. So, as Christ taught it, his followers should have the ability to grow, to flex, to be shaped by fresh ideas from the living Word of God. I think Hoss demonstrated that, too.

- Summer jobs—does this still exist? It was common in my youth. Snagging a job at a grocery store, working at the swimming pool, or assisting a commercial fisherman (all of which I did) put you in the money!

- Churches of Christ. I introduce this church in this chapter because this beautiful body of believers has been my home since that baptism day, and there is no way I could tell my story without it. I have now served over 40 years in ministry within this fellowship. Much has changed, but much has not. I love this church. I have been supported, blessed, encouraged, and formed through it. We are far from a perfect bunch. Our history is both unique and perplexing. But we are still here, growing by the grace of God.

- Numerous excellent and enjoyable resources bring the "Restoration Movement" back to life if you want to know more about us and our history. This is the period in the 19th century that formed us. Out of that movement, with its desire to follow the Bible alone, came both Churches of Christ and Christian Churches. One excellent resource I recommend is *The Encyclopedia of the Stone/Campbell Movement*, published by William B. Eerdmans Publishing Company.

- As I mentioned, baptism is a hallmark teaching of the Churches of Christ. Sometimes, throughout our history, this emphasis has been so strong that it seems to eclipse other biblical teachings. But baptism has a firm biblical foundation (see Matthew 28:19-20; Acts 2:38; Acts 8:26-40; Acts 22:16; Romans 6:3-4, to name a few), and we continue to encourage baptism for every believer who comes to faith in Jesus. It is a significant milestone of faith and of life. For many, their baptism date is as important to commemorate as their birthdate.

Fully Integrated

When I arrived, Magnolia Bible College (MBC) was just a fledgling school in Kosciusko. Having started the year before, it was finding its way as I was finding mine. It was and remained a small school with a narrow focus. The only degrees offered were in Bible and Ministry, but as a full four-year college, classes in other endeavors were also required. As a testimony to its faculty and staff, MBC eventually earned full accreditation with the national Southern Association of Colleges and Schools (SACS)—the smallest college ever to accomplish this. But this high academic standard had yet to be achieved in my first couple of years there.

It was more like a family atmosphere. The campus was shared with the local Church of Christ. It was a perfect environment for me as a young man and a young Christian. I did not care much for math and science, but I enjoyed every minute of the Bible-focused classes. I settled into the rhythm of class and work at Central Office Supply, which would be my life for the next four years. Over those years, I met many new people and developed friendships I continue to enjoy.

The "Mansion" was the only dorm then. It was a large, old house located adjacent to the campus, with every room converted into a dorm room, including the dining area. A collection of us young aspiring preacher boys was packed into it. Some of us were white, and some were black. It was an interesting mix from all over Mississippi and beyond, guys from all backgrounds. As much as anything else, life in the Mansion became my teacher.

Of course, I brought my passion with me—still burning intensely to convert the world, but I was still a farm-fresh Christian. I knew little compared to some of the other guys who had grown up in Churches of Christ. However, as I acquired knowledge through my classes and studies, the more I knew, the more I thought I knew. I was not alone in this, however. The Mansion became a hotbed of theological discourse. To use that phrase again, all sorts of mental gymnastics broke out between us. It was all in good fun, but beyond the moment, none of us took it too seriously.

ROOSEVELT

Well, except maybe one. His name was Roosevelt Johnson. If asked how he was doing, he always answered, "I am just naturally happy, can't you see?" He was my roommate for a time. He hailed from Columbus, Mississippi, and was reared in a very strict Church of Christ home. He had a rather impressive "Afro" or "natural" hairstyle. He seemed to have a wealth of biblical knowledge, even if I thought his approach was relatively narrow. He even disparaged playing cards, something I could not comprehend. He was a serious young man. While I lacked nothing in zeal, I could also be anything but serious. To Roosevelt, I often was "a clown" (his term), but we managed to co-exist. He was an athlete, and we bonded over the basketball court and the Lord despite our differences as we settled into our new home in the Mansion and grew in our desire to serve the Lord.

We certainly talked about race, about the differences between the black and white churches, and about why that kind of segregation still existed. As our Bible Studies were leading us, we began to more clearly understand that God was no respecter of persons (see Acts 10:34) and that His church should be reflective of that. We both agreed that if we were ever in charge, that would all change. And, honestly, we thought we should be put in charge—somewhere, anyway. After all, we surely knew as much about it as our professors!

GROWTH

Since MBC was an upstart school with small class populations, our opportunities to learn from our professors extended outside the classroom. It sounds very much like a cliché, but we were like one big family. We were able to spend quality time with our professors in various settings, learning invaluable lessons away from academics. We went on those door-to-door campaigns together, played tennis, ate together regularly, and became friends. Many of those professors still impact me decades later.

One was Dr. Bill Lambert, whom we called "Brother Grace" due to his liberal grading curves, especially in Greek class. He certainly gave us what *we needed* instead of what *we deserved*. He was a gentle giant of faith to us preacher boys. He had been in ministry his entire adult life, and we marveled at his stories of church life—some wonderful, but others not as much. Besides in homiletics, it was precisely the kind of training we needed.

Another person we all admired was Dr. Cecil May, Jr. He was the second MBC president and fully brought to the college the academic focus that ushered in the accreditation. Dr. May brought a crucial balance between academics and practical ministry that became the college's foundation. He served there for almost two decades and has influenced generations of preachers in our tribe.

Bill and Cecil went from MBC to other universities to bless other students. Both are now retired but remain ever with a specific vintage of MBC alums. As life happens, I work on the same church staff with Cecil May III, his son and fellow MBC grad. I am unsure if I could have had a better incubator for my faith or any better training for ministry other than what that tiny school in the middle of Mississippi provided. My faith and knowledge grew by leaps and bounds there, and I am forever grateful.

BLACK AND WHITE

My horizons increased across a broad spectrum while at MBC, including in matters of race. Besides Roosevelt, there was Willie, James, Stanley, Garfield, Johnny, Curtis, and many other black students, most of whom remain in ministry and are life-long friends. I lived with them, hung out with them, studied with them, and worshipped with them. One of the perks of being a preacher boy student at MBC was the opportunity to visit churches all across the state and occasionally even preach. I took full advantage on every occasion.

Some of my fondest memories were participating in what was then called a "Fellowship Day." These occurred almost exclusively within the black churches. They would begin with regular Sunday morning study and worship activities, followed by a lavish lunch known as a "fellowship meal" provided by the good ladies of the congregation and then continued after that with several speakers delivering short five-minute presentations, concluding with a longer sermon offered by the most senior minister. It was an all-day affair, and I ate it up—the teaching and the food. Eventually, I was even allowed to be one of those five-minute speakers. That was a thrill—to hear the support returning from the church, fully accepting me in my feeble efforts. I never gave much thought to the fact that I was hanging out mostly in black churches, but others had noticed.

One of the printers at Central Office Supply always

made it a habit to ask me where I had been the previous Sunday. After a while of listening to my answers, he asked me why I was spending so much time in black churches. Weren't there white churches I could attend? Of course, I took offense at that, challenging him back on why I shouldn't participate in worship in black churches. One Monday, after recalling the day before with him, telling him about a fellowship day I enjoyed, he asked me if I had lunched with that church. Upon hearing my affirmation, he paused, then curtly remarked, "You would never find me eating with N...!" My reply back was just as sharp and pointed. "Well, if you are in Christ, color does not matter, so that must mean you are not in Christ!" I bellowed loudly, with zero thought of tact. I could tell he was affected as my words hung in the air. I was not sure how, but he was. After that, we stopped talking about my Sundays. A couple of years later, he reminded me of that conversation when I was about to graduate and move on to my first full-time church. He recalled that my words had hurt him, but they also made him think about his racist views. Back then, I was a blunt instrument for the Lord, but despite my arrogance, God protected me from myself and even somehow worked through it. It should have humbled me, but more often than not, it just emboldened me. I had learned a lot of new information, but *grace* remained largely undiscovered.

A CONFRONTATION

Someone else who noticed was one of the college administrators. He approached me—not out of the same concerns as the printer—but he wanted me to broaden my scope to include more churches. Through his urging and connections, I traveled across Mississippi, visiting and sometimes preaching in the small Churches of Christ that dotted the state. On one such occasion, I again saw first-hand the ugliness of racism and why the church remained segregated.

It was a country church—one, like so many, that had been established in the earlier part of the twentieth century, flourished for a while, but now was on the back-side of their glory days. I was visiting that morning to represent the Bible College as a student. I had accompanied one of the staff members in MBC's ongoing effort to keep the congregations informed of its mission to educate and train men for ministry within Churches of Christ, especially in Mississippi. We had enjoyed the worship, appealed for our mission, and were about to leave when several cars tore into the parking lot. I can still hear the screeching wheels. It was the beginning of winter when the battle between cold, dry air and warm, humid air started. On this day, the warm, moist air was gaining ground. Clouds hung low, but rain had not yet arrived. So, when those cars peeled into the gravel parking lot, a dust cloud hovered over the scene, creating a surreal moment reminiscent of a horror movie.

And it was horrible. Shock does not begin to describe it. Several men jumped from the cars with faces red from anger and seemingly out for blood. Jerry, the MBC staffer, and I stood there, then backed away. The target of these outraged men was the preacher of that church. They surrounded him, forming a circle. Harsh words and accusations flew. I could not relate it to anything I had ever known. It was the antithesis of what should be expected at church. As we soon discovered, it all centered around the fact that this preacher had baptized a black person in the church's baptistry.

Someone recognized that these men were church

members who had boycotted that morning's worship to demonstrate their opposition and displeasure. Instead, they chose to ambush the preacher after worship. Threats were thrown the preacher's way. Nasty racist terms were repeated over and over to the encircled preacher. To his credit, he did not back down; however, we later learned that he did lose his job. As a still young preacher boy witnessing all of this—it was unbelievable and outrageous. How could these men call themselves Christians and act in this manner? My instinct was to jump into the fray, spout some Bible verses, and set these men straight. Understanding the volatility of the situation, Jerry wisely prevented that. Just recalling this dusty, unpleasant scene makes my heart sad. The angry men finally left.

It fully demonstrated to me that outside of my little Bible College existence, racism was fully alive and well, even in the church. It was one thing for a printer—a church outsider—to air out his racist dirty laundry, but seeing it play out in real-time at church, well, that was a heartbreaker. Yet that was still the reality in some sections of Mississippi in the late 1970s, but certainly not all.

BACK TO GREENVILLE

On occasion, I would get back to Greenville. The South Main church fully supported my efforts to prepare for ministry, and one of their beloved shepherds, Dr. Blaylock, had invited me to preach to the congregation after a time. I was thrilled but also nervous. These folks had known me since I was a small child. My family would be in attendance. But I was determined to give it my best. I can still see my grandfather—the longtime Church of Christ stalwart—sitting in the pew, using the hearing device installed for him and shedding tears as I preached along.

Ma Whit's face looked proud and joyful as she listened. Of course, my sermon included blistering referendums on race and fully integrating churches, but it went well. The church there loved me and continued to support me throughout my education. I owe a great deal to them, not the least of which is their patience in putting up with my self-assuredness.

THE WALL REMAINED

Life, study, work, classes, and visits to churches all over the state continued for me in Kosciusko, relatively uninterrupted over the next few years. MBC was growing in both students and reputation. The Mansion remained full but often with different faces. At one point, I became the lone white face in it. I learned what life was like as a minority! We shared life, debated obscure points of theology, got on each other's nerves, and grew together.

One of Magnolia Bible College's legacies I cherish most is the professors who taught us to think independently. Sure, they were instilling within us the traditional teachings and doctrinal approach to Scripture developed over decades within Churches of Christ, but along with that, they urged us to study the Bible on our own, learn healthy habits in our studies, and most of all, develop our own faith and understanding of the Bible. That has served me quite well over the years, as it has my peers, many of whom remain engaged in full-time ministry in their communities. None of us are now who we were then, but none of us would be who we are now without those distant experiences.

Eventually, I moved out of the Mansion and lived with a couple of other guys in an apartment during my senior year. Other preacher boys—guys like Leslie, John, Les,

Cecil, and Tim—became as close to me as brothers and have remained so ever since. Through it all, I could never escape that invisible wall's presence. Even though my life had become fully integrated and some progress had been made in a few churches (the campus church in Kosciusko was integrated), the racial and cultural divides that separated blacks and whites for centuries continued. No actual doors with "white" and "colored" above them existed anymore, but the idea behind those doors did. However, I have learned in the many years that followed that tearing down this wall is not as simple as I once thought.

Back then, my solution was to preach a sermon—educate, indict, call for change from a biblical text, and expect immediate results. If only. The problem is much too deeply rooted for this. As I traveled Mississippi, visiting and preaching as a student preacher, I would occasionally encounter someone who would express concern to me about the number of black students at MBC. In response, I would express how this should not be an area of concern but a reason to rejoice. These incidents only served to remind me how entrenched racism remained. Other times, however, I was met with voices supporting MBC's effort to reach into black churches for students. Therefore, I witnessed changes in attitudes and actions, if ever so slowly. I was thankful for it. Maybe some progress was being made. That reminded me that the wall was not nearly as impenetrable and ominous as it once seemed.

MEMORIES AND MORE:

- Like many Mississippi towns and small cities, Kosciusko is not the same place as in my college days. The "Beehive of the Hills" and the childhood home of Oprah Winfrey does not seem to be buzzing at the same level now, although the square remains the center of town. Many, if not most, of the businesses and industries to which I delivered office supplies no longer exist. But some have been replaced by newer industry, and Kosciusko, sitting as it does on the Natchez Trace, is still an inviting, charming, small southern town.

- Magnolia Bible College closed its doors permanently in December 2009. Economic realities finally caught up, and finding funds and support for such a small, narrowly focused institution became too difficult. For most of us associated with the college, its closing was heartbreaking. It was a blessing to the Churches of Christ in Mississippi and beyond for over thirty-five years. The campus remains around the Huntington Church of Christ (itself smaller than it once was). MBC, at its zenith, represented some of the best within our fellowship—a desire to train future generations in ministry, a dedication to biblical teaching, a balanced approach between doctrine and practice, a genuine love for the Lord, and a desire to grow his kingdom. I still lament the passing of MBC, but it remains alive in the hearts and minds of everyone fortunate to be a part of it.
- Mississippi certainly deserves its racial reputation based on history, as I witnessed forty-plus years ago, but things have changed. It is rather lazy and somewhat irresponsible to

label the Magnolia State with the broad brush of racism now. Churches of Christ have also come a long way in this regard, with numerous congregations (including South Main in Greenville) integrated. It is progress that should be celebrated.

- Preaching in black congregations was a pleasure. Their vocal support of preaching is always a joy. The "amens" and "that's right" from the congregation encourage every preacher. Typically, at least back in my college days, black churches did not enjoy the same resources as white churches, so it was more difficult for them to sustain a full-time local preacher, but they gave what they had. On one preaching visit to a black church in North Mississippi, this was evident to me. After my sermon, a church leader addressed the congregation, expressing thanksgiving for my visit and appreciation for the word spoken. He then challenged the congregation to express their gratitude as well. So, the collection trays were passed out for the second time that Sunday and my honorarium became that collection—their "love offering" was handed to me in a bag. I remember this over and above many other honorariums I have received in more traditional forms. It was a personal expression of thanksgiving for the place of preaching in churches.

7

Oak Ridge

Besides the campus church, there were four other congregations of Churches of Christ in Attala County, of which Kosciusko is the county seat. Two were white, and two were black. All were small struggling groups scattered among the gently rolling hills and back country roads so prevalent in central Mississippi.

One of those congregations was Oak Ridge. It was tucked away in a holler on a gravel road (a "holler" is a spot around the next corner and down the hill). It was a tiny church of around 25 people. They met in an old shotgun, Masonite-sided church building featuring a small sanctuary attached to two smaller classrooms. Inside, near the ancient, creaky pews, stood a couple of space heaters to tame the winter frost and one air conditioner mounted in a window to ease the summer heat (and without fail also to provide housing for wasps each spring). One noticeably absent feature, however, was plumbing. But, no problem, the outhouse was only a brisk walk away, down a path beside the building, and it worked just fine.

I first visited the Oak Ridge Church of Christ as a part of a class field trip. One of our professors—teaching us about the origins of Churches of Christ—thought it would benefit us to travel to each congregation in the county and learn of their interconnected history. It was a welcome diversion, anything to get out of the classroom! Earlier, I mentioned the Restoration Movement and its significance to Churches of Christ. This was like a current event in congregations like Oak Ridge, though it began well over a century before. All the original leaders of that movement's first and second generations were deceased, but the connections were strong. These congregations were still filled with people whose parents and grandparents personally knew some of the Restoration leaders. Some of these pioneer preachers had visited these churches. Entire congregation's DNAs could be traced back to the faithful work of those men and women. Oak Ridge was such a place where the names, reputations, and teachings of the faithful of old continued to live.

As we rolled up on the small church building, we saw the cemetery across the road. This was and remains a common site throughout the rural South, with folks even now being born, married, and buried all within close proximity to their home church. What stands out the most about that visit to "the Ridge" (a name we preacher boys would eventually affectionally tag this church) was a question by the professor. He asked us which of the two—the church or the cemetery—had more life in them. The little church was an easy target because it was seemingly slowly fading away with an aging membership. On the surface, it did not have much going for it.

But I would learn better. Not long after this trip, I became the part-time preacher for the Ridge. I began what, in effect, became a ministry for this church—patiently putting up with pitiful sermons, shaky homiletics, and self-assured theological discourses by a string of MBC preacher boys. There certainly was life there for us as we practiced our craft on these willing subjects.

It put us in the real world of a church—no longer was it merely theory; no longer were we one-hit wonders, rolling into a church as a guest student preacher repeating our memorized sermon. No, this was our introduction to the weekly grind of producing new sermons and classes. I will admit to not always being up to production standards. Along the way, I discovered the secret resource of sermon outline books, and not just on one occasion did I resort to the lazy shortcut of ripping a page out of one of the books a few minutes before arriving to preach! The Ridge holds a special place in my heart. Those good folks gave me my start.

LIFE ON THE FARM

One of the entrenched leaders within that little flock was Brother Clay. If an old school existed before the old school, Clay attended it. His wardrobe consisted of faded overalls for casual attire and newer Sunday-go-to-meeting overalls for church and other formal gatherings. He was balding and round—the latter a consequence of his wife, Miss Helen's incredible culinary skills. He had been a logger, then a sawmill operator. He had limited formal education but knew his way around a forest and a farm. He and Helen lived on such a farm.

Over time, this farm became, to me, somewhat like the tugboat on Lake Ferguson, a place for adventure and wonder. This way of life was all new to me: chasing cows back into the pasture, gathering eggs from the laying hens, hanging slaughtered hogs in the smokehouse so the meat could cure, picking fresh tomatoes from the vine, exploring and fishing the creek that ran back behind the barn where the water was clear, something unseen in the Delta.

They had raised their family there—some were still close to home and a part of the Ridge. When I came on the scene, Clay was retired, caring for the cattle, hogs, and chickens, carefully tending to the expansive vegetable garden. It was unlike my experience growing up in Greenville, and I loved it. I became close to them as Helen delighted in watching the spectacle of me and Brother Clay demolish her excellent cooking. To this day, I have never experienced anything like her coconut cake.

LIFE IN A CHURCH

At Oak Ridge, I discovered the unwelcome world of inner church politics. There was another prominent leader among that small flock. His name was Marvin, and he was also the song leader for the church. He loved leading the church each Sunday in such old, venerated hymns as *Amazing Grace* and *When the Roll is Called Up Yonder*. He was a pleasant guy—always quick with a joke, but he and Clay were friendly rivals, but rivals, nonetheless. When it came time for significant decisions, Clay would ensure those loyal to his way of thinking attended the pivotal decision-making meeting. Marvin would do the same. As a young preacher, I had to figure out how to navigate this—lessons that have benefited me throughout my ministry.

As you might imagine, I ruffled a few feathers as I navigated. At one point, Marvin contacted the chairman of the board of trustees at the college, recommending that I should be encouraged to seek out another vocation! On another occasion, I angered an older couple who, while able to do most everything else, hardly ever felt well enough to attend any church service. On a visit, whatever I said as I encouraged them to return to worship was interpreted as an accusation that their "sickness was just in their head." They huffed and puffed about it to others, including Helen, who said maybe I had a point. Interestingly enough, we began to see more of them on Sundays.

As the days passed, I spent more time with Clay and Helen. The continual invitations to lunch certainly helped. One of Clay's favorite snacks was Helen's leftover sausage biscuits smothered in mustard, which I also enjoyed. I also learned how much Clay enjoyed professional wrestling, how he disdained washing clothes on a Sunday (it was the

Sabbath, after all, and a day of rest), how he enjoyed eating the smallish, redeye bass (or "Cyprus Trout" as he called them) I caught out of their creek, and how incredibly he had once known my grandfather—Ma Whit's husband.

FAMILY CONNECTIONS

After several conversations, we connected all the dots. My maternal grandfather had been a school teacher in rural Attala County decades before. Clay called up his memory of an "old man Whittington," not only being one of his teachers in such a school but also being swift with discipline. As a kid, he remembered seeing my grandfather with a woman and a young child (Ma Whit and her oldest son, my eventual uncle Al). That was a fantastic connection that bonded me even more closely to them. Happily, he and Ma Whit, along with my mother, Eleanor, met after I graduated from MBC. That, too, is a cherished memory.

THE NOT-SO-INVISIBLE WALL

The "old school" came out in Clay in numerous ways —one was in his attitude toward black people. Clay was a product of his environment and social conditioning. I never sensed deep hatred in him toward black people; it was more like distrust and fear combined with a belief that the races should be kept separate. Of course, it was a belief born out of ignorance, but Clay seemed unmovable. To him, the wall was not invisible at all.

We engaged in numerous discussions about it. Clay would go to several Old Testament verses to prove his point. It says, "Come from among them and be ye separate," he would emphasize in the good English of the King James Version of the Bible. In response, I quickly pointed out that he was misapplying those texts and using them out of their original context in a way never imagined when written—twisting them to support his narrative. I would then share with him several New Testament Scriptures on how God was no respecter of persons. Helen would sit quietly by, taking it all in, occasionally interrupting when Clay got a tad rowdy, even chiding him by saying, "Now Clay, you know Danny is right." It became an ongoing exercise that, for some reason, Clay usually initiated.

However, all of it came to a head outside of that discussion as plans for a county-wide "door knocking" campaign of MBC staff and students were announced. Spring break every year at MBC consisted of such a campaign. Students, faculty, and staff would load up and head out to support a church's efforts in a Mississippi town or community. All the arrangements would have been pre-made; then, we would show up, go into selected neighborhoods, and invite people to visit the church and study the Bible. Overall, it was usually a positive experience, mainly met with cordial responses from those we contacted and greatly appreciated by the local church. However, This particular spring, instead of traveling away for the campaign, we stayed home. The plan was to spend one day in support of each of the five Churches of Christ in Attala County—using the college's resources of people to go into the surrounding neighborhoods of these churches, extending invitations for them. The offer came through me to the Oak Ridge congregation.

It did not set well with Clay. It was apparent he was troubled from the outset, but since otherwise, it was met with approval, he went along. It was not hard to notice that he became more visibly irritated as time drew closer to the

MBC invasion. Finally, he confronted me on the Wednesday night before everyone arrived on Friday. He wanted to know if "those black boys" would be a part of the campaign group. After hearing my affirmation, he demanded that I put a stop to it; "go back and tell them that they are not welcome here," he uttered. Even though I knew of his prejudicial leanings, I was not expecting this. It caught me briefly off-guard, but I recovered. In reply, I expressed that I would do no such thing, how I could not believe what I was hearing from him, and if he did not want them to participate, he could tell them himself on Friday when we all arrived.

When I returned to the Mansion that night, I relayed this story to the other guys—one of whom was Roosevelt. Of course, he was planning to be in the campaign group, but after hearing about Clay, he also decided upon an additional mission. He asked me to identify Clay upon our arrival. He determined to walk up to Clay and offer his hand. I thought it was a marvelous plan. I did not know what might happen or if Clay would even be there, but he was. I braced myself about what might occur, but Clay accepted Roosevelt extended his hand. Introductions were made over the handshake, and that was that. The door-knocking efforts went as planned, as did a fabulous meal the Oak Ridge ladies provided afterward. Nothing between Clay and me was spoken about it afterward. Occasionally, we returned to our discussions about race, but life went much as before. Little did I realize how impactful these moments were for Clay.

CRACKS IN THE WALL

Years later, after I had been in preaching ministry for some time, I was asked to return to the Ridge for a revival

—to preach a gospel meeting for them. Gladly, I accepted this invitation, in no small part, because I would be hosted by Clay and Helen, and visions of her dinner table were an irresistible incentive. Not long after I settled in at their house, Clay indicated he wanted to talk with me. It was as if no time had passed since our previous conversations together. Clay had a way of swiping down across his face with his hand, followed by a big sigh before he spoke about something important to him. This he did and then got directly to the point—so much so that, at first, he lost me completely. He stated to me, "You were right." As lovely as it always is to hear someone affirm you, you still want to know what you were right about. So, I asked him. His reply was totally unexpected. He continued, "About those black boys, you were right." He did not have to say anymore. Even though it had been years, I knew exactly what he meant. Words escaped me in the moment. I could not respond. Even now, it brings back the happy emotions of the moment. He had been carrying this around since our days together—eager now to unburden. This "old school" man, now well into his eighties, born into and shaped by embedded Mississippi racist culture, had wrestled with the devil over this, eventually allowing God to soften his heart to the point he could now confess the error of his ways. It was an overwhelming moment for him, Helen (who was crying), and me. I will never be able to forget the look on Clay's face as he released years of spite and prejudice.

Please don't misunderstand; Clay was no social justice pioneer and no hero ahead of his time. No, not even close. Actually, he would have been considered a dinosaur even then, but this was no minor adjustment from him. Coming from where he had been to where he arrived, even if it was an extended journey, demonstrated to me that there is always hope for a better day and that God, when given an opening, can work through even the thickest skin and hardest heart to bring about change; to break down that wall further.

I think of this story quite often now, in light of our current social unrest, as accusations and labels fly, as hatred abounds, as one unfortunate event after another continues to demonstrate that we, after all of these years, have not overcome that much. I think if Clay could get there, we all can! If God can perform that kind of miracle in a tiny church in the outback of Mississippi, he can perform it in the heart of our major cities as well. We must listen to him and get ourselves out of the way, much like Clay eventually did.

Clay and Helen are now buried in that cemetery at Oak Ridge. Even when I knew them, they were remnants from a previous era—some have been tagged as the greatest generation. They typically came by things the hard way with lots of labor and determined work. Clay came to his late-in-life realization that way also. But make no mistake—it was a God thing. Only God could have led him out of that wilderness.

That remains just as true now. It is not politicians, legislation, laws, rioting, special-interest groups, or anything that emerges from Washington, D.C., that will erase hatred, prejudice, and all the evil that goes with it. That should be apparent to us as all continue to fail us spectacularly. It has to be a God thing. Only he can lead us out of hatred, prejudice, and racism. I pray that we, somehow, give him that chance.

After I moved away into my first full-time preaching work, Oak Ridge continued to offer Magnolia Bible College students the opportunity to practice on them. (I cannot imagine how many sad sermons have been spoken there). I have Oak Ridge in common now with several friends who knew Clay, enjoyed Helen's cooking, and got their first taste of church ministry at the Ridge. Amazingly, this wonderful little church is still around in an expanded, renovated building (including plumbing) with a new generation of people populating it. I guess it had more life than that professor could ever have dreamed.

MEMORIES AND MORE:

- As I previously mentioned, old church cemeteries are common in the south. Just drive through the countryside; chances are you will venture upon one. Most of the folks I know have a loved one buried in an old church cemetery somewhere. Often, these are a source of pride for the church, especially if a local well-known preacher or notable person is buried there. While preaching at Oak Ridge, I helped dig a grave—not uncommon for it to be a community project, as everyone pitched in. In the Bible I used then, there is an inscription copied from an Oak Ridge gravestone, which I still use occasionally when officiating a funeral. It goes like this: "Remember me as you pass by. As you are now, so once was I. As I am now, so you must be. Prepare for death and follow me."
- Today, it seems to have become relatively easy to dismiss the old, country-type folks, living as they do more "off the grid." they seem much less sophisticated than ever, considering our tech world. They are the folks in the fly-over

part of the nation—thought to be a little backward. Such is a mischaracterization. Perhaps rural people are not as tech-savvy and live a tad slower pace. Still, from my experience, these folks are the backbone of our nation and, indeed, the backbone of our churches, faithfully following Christ while handing their faith down to the next generations. They may have the reputation of being rigid and, as we say in the South, "set in their ways," but as Clay demonstrated, that is not the entire story. Besides the Oak Ridge congregation, I also had the privilege to serve in another rural church in North Mississippi—the Pine Grove Church of Christ in Fulton. I fondly remember those years with these good folks doing their best to glorify God. Without these types of dedicated, hard-working people, there likely would not be a fellowship of Churches of Christ. No, they are not perfect, but they never claim to be. And they certainly have blessed my life.

- Jesus shared a story, "The Parable of the Sower," in Matthew 13:1-23. In it, Jesus identifies different soil types in relation to planting seeds. Some soil is fertile, ready to receive the seed, allowing its deep roots to grow into a mature plant. Other soils work to prevent such growth due to impediments within. The soil in this story represents different kinds of hearts—some are receptive to the Word of God and take it in sincerely, forming themselves around this heavenly seed. Other hearts can become hardened and distracted, never giving

God's Word much of an opportunity to make an impact. I think of Clay when I read this parable. I think of the patience of God and the power of his Word to penetrate. It is all a process. Seeds grow differently—some slower than others according to the soil, but if we hang in there with the Lord, his seeds will bear fruit in our lives, even enabling us to overcome a lifetime of prejudice. Yes, the seeds of God's kingdom can produce vines that will run all over that invisible wall, then grow into maturity and bring it down.

- God has allowed me to travel over quite a bit of the world. I have tasted zeppelini in Lithuania (the national dish—boiled potatoes that were then blanched, filled with meat, cheese, or sauce, and then fashioned into the shape of a blimp or zeppelin); fine French cuisine in Paris; fresh calamari in a coastal Greek village; jerked chicken in the Caribbean; farm-fresh pineapple in Honduras; tasty warm apple strudel in Germany; fresh-out-of-the oven pizza in Italy; and crawfish jambalaya in New Orleans. But honestly, nothing quite compares to the fresh sweet corn, vine-ripened tomatoes, fried (yes!) okra, just-shelled speckled butter beans, sautéed squash, and onion, along with buttered cornbread, sweet tea, and sweet potato pie served on the tables of country folks from Oak Ridge or Pine Grove.

- Speaking of food, have you ever experienced a church "dinner on the grounds?" This vanishing tradition was sometimes connected to the church cemetery. At Pine Grove, we had an annual "Decoration Day," when families would return to put fresh flowers on graves and remember loved ones. On that Sunday, vast amounts of food were stacked on tables lined up in the churchyard. Everyone then enjoyed "dinner on the grounds." It was amazing.

8

Tearing Down The Wall?

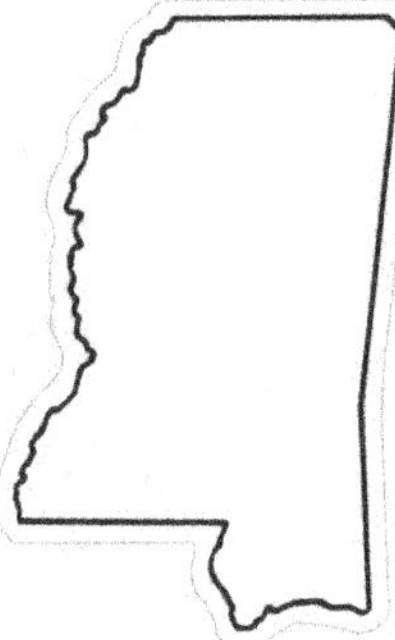

Since those Oak Ridge days, God has led me on quite a journey, frequently far from my Mississippi roots. My path has taken me across Europe to the Baltic country of Lithuania, down into Central and South America, to see biblical geographical sites in Greece and Israel, to the Florida panhandle, and now to central Arkansas. All along the way, there have been reminders that we still have much work to do if that *invisible wall* is to crumble.

I recognized this during my ministry at the Skyway Hills Church of Christ in Pearl, Mississippi, near the capital city of Jackson. During this time, the church was thriving, growing, and expanding. We successfully reached out to a wide variety of people in our community, with one exception being the African-American community. We were an integrated church, but just barely. Wayne and Pam Hervey, and their daughters blessed that church with vibrant, infectious faith and plentiful energy. All by himself, Wayne, with his mega-watt smile and outsized personality, likely tore down the wall in several hearts within that congregation. Together, we devised a plan to reach out to Wayne and Pam's rural, primarily black neighborhood to invite them to our church. We asked a black college friend and colleague, Johnny Beckwith, who then had a tent ministry (he would go into communities, set up his tent, and preach over a few nights). We got it all set up. Johnny came, and we had overflowing crowds each night. But it never translated into any lasting connection to our church. Wayne later informed me that the feedback he got from his neighbors mainly was doubt and suspicion. One statement he passed along summed it up. He was told, "Why are those white folks in our neighborhood? What do they want from us?" It was that *invisible wall* again. Even when you think it is absent, it reappears.

INTERNATIONAL WALLS

It even existed in the central European country of Lithuania. Beginning in 1996, I have been traveling to this beautiful country on the Baltic Sea, which ultimately led to my wife, Terri, and I, along with our oldest daughter, Taylor, living there as resident missionaries for a few years right after the turn of the 21st century. I genuinely love this place and its people. Known for its exceptional basketball play, abundant amber, and natural beauty, it has emerged from the Cold War shadow of the Soviet Union into a vibrant, thriving, independent country. But I could not help but notice that even though the iron curtain fell, walls between people remained. I heard numerous times the all-to-familiar refrains of prejudicial language expressed. It was not about black and white there but about Lithuanian and Russian. Many Lithuanians despised the Russian population and said so in no uncertain terms. Many Russians resented the Lithuanians and their independence. This was common in all of the Baltic states, even leading to violence on occasion.

But I also did see racial stereotyping towards black people there, too. Vilnius is Lithuania's capital city. It literally sparkles today. Typically, it is overflowing now with tourists from all over the world—walking the colorful streets of the Old Town or visiting the ancient site of Gediminas Tower (Grand Duke Gediminas for Lithuanians would be the equivalent of our George Washington). Back some time ago, while it was still in this transition to this modern city, I had the occasion to walk with a group of lively teenagers on Gediminas Prospectus—the main street of the city connecting the marvelous City Cathedral on one end to the historic national Parliament building on the other. Once, in the basement of a government building along this street, people were tortured and killed who dared resist the Soviet way. A KGB museum there now preserves in chilling detail the horrors of that persecution. Today, you can visit this museum and then stop in for a Quarter Pounder with Cheese a few blocks away.

On that sunny but cold March day ahead of our group was a black man—a rare sight in the early stages after their independence. He was the first black person these teenagers had ever seen in person. They were animated, talking about him. In her innocence and ignorance, one girl asked if it would be okay to approach him and touch his skin (not the best idea I counseled). Another expressed fear, thinking he might harm us. As we discussed their reaction, old, well-worn stereotypes about black people were offered up. Having no experience with black people, these kids were regurgitating bits and pieces of racist propaganda they had picked up—even if they were unaware of it. It surprised me, but I realized that the invisible wall separating black and white extended across Europe.

In Florida, the Gateway Church of Christ enjoyed a racially diverse congregation, but it was still a majority white church—as is the church where I now serve, the Levy Church of Christ, in North Little Rock, Arkansas. In both churches, we enjoy wonderful community and fellowship, working together to tear the wall down, but it is stubborn. After all, it has been carefully built over the years with resistant, hard-to-penetrate material.

LEVY

This was illustrated by an unfortunate and tragic event that unfolded mere yards away from the Levy campus on an early frigid January morning. Out of a traffic stop, a young black man was shot and killed by police. The back-lash to this was immediate, particularly in the local black community. Hundreds rallied directly in front of and on our campus to support the family. Before the police released the camera footage, strong statements were made, including how the shooting (the police officers were white) was racially motivated, but also how the young man was merely a "thug" who deserved what he got (Racism thrives in ignorance). As we interacted and opened up our facilities to the family and supporters, I talked to a lawyer from Chicago. He shared that he had not yet met the family but was here to make someone in authority pay for this unjust act. Later, after the complete camera footage was released, it showed clearly that the young man did produce a weapon first, firing at the officers. Still, some continued to use this tragedy as a platform to create increased tension between whites and blacks. And it came from every side as our church received anonymous letters and phone calls threatening us if we did not remove the small cross, flow-ers, stuffed animals, along with other items left on our campus at the spot of the shooting by the young man's family and friends. Within these threats was laced the N-word. I was proud of our church throughout all of this. We hosted the funeral of the young man. We also were sensi-tive to those within our church who serve in law enforce-ment (none were involved in the shooting). We did our best to serve the family and our community while navigating the rhetoric, anger, confusion, accusations, and hurt surrounding it. The wall, while not seen, was felt through it all.

THE POWER OF ACCUSATIONS

Now, as I watch similar scenes sadly repeated with too

much frequency all across our land, I wonder if healing can happen, that is, if we will allow it to happen. According to news reports filling our screens daily, it does not seem as if we are making much progress. It is as if the wall is rebuilding itself.

It takes me back to Washington Avenue in Greenville—to those protesters in front of Stein Mart. So much has happened since then, but here we see another generation of protest. Numerous civil rights legislations have become law since then. We elected a black president. Our congress is currently more racially diverse than ever before in history. Yet here we are again. Accusations continue to fly. The wall remains and threatens to be the dividing point of the 21st century.

Could there be a single sinister force behind it all? A force that is not interested in the least about racial harmony and reconciliation? No, I am not about to float out a conspiracy theory about shadowy government forces, but shadowy is an apt description. He does operate in the darkness to accomplish his agenda. And he is all about fostering accusations, strife, discontentment, and division. I am speaking of Satan—of the devil himself. Now, before you react or roll your eyes, stay with me on this and allow me to offer you a biblical perspective.

THE FATHER OF LIES

Satan is exposed in the Bible as "the father of all lies" (John 8:44). His currency is temptation—playing on our weaknesses and fears, exploiting them for his purposes of creating chaos, anger, and hurt. His goal is "only to kill, steal and destroy" (John 10:10). One of the primary weapons in his arsenal is accusations. The Bible outs him plainly as "the accuser" (Revelation 12:10). The Greek word from which "accuser" is translated is also rooted in another English word—category. In New Testament times, Christians were accused of incredible crimes, such as incest (misunderstanding of the terms "brother" and "sister" within the church context had outsiders believing that biological siblings were married to each other), cannibalism (another misunderstanding about the language and practice of communion), and burning down Rome (Emperor Nero's accusation). They were categorized as "atheists" because they did not believe in the Roman pantheon of gods. All of this was used as ammunition to marginalize and demonize them, creating an atmosphere of suspicion and hatred, leading to both physical and economic persecution. Satan weaponized accusations, and it worked. Thousands of Christians were martyred for their faith.

Another historical example of this is Nazi Germany. How could otherwise sensible German people not only accept but participate in the mass murder of millions of their fellow citizens? Indeed, it did not happen overnight, but only after years of repeated accusations of labeling Jewish people sub-human, as the source of all German woes, and categorizing them as expendable. Eventually, many Germans believed the lies fostered by the accusations and even saw the Jewish extermination as a positive step forward for their Fatherland. This is how thoroughly the accuser does his work.

He is working hard in our country now, sowing the same seeds of discontentment and stirring up anger and hatred with every accusatory headline and social media post. The goal is to say something long enough and loud enough until we believe it and then look for someone to blame. Even when the worst headlines are accurate, the accuser's way will not lead us to any solution or healing.

The continued politicizing of race will not eradicate that wall. It will only reinforce it and create more accusations, bitterness, separation, and violence.

This is why I am convinced that permanent solutions will not be found in our political system. If so, it should have happened by now. Racism seems too embedded in hearts to be legislated out. With each new awful incident, we seem to fall into the same vicious cycle of accusations, blame, violence, hurt, harm, and outrage with very little progress. But there is another way—and it will not come from within us alone. Martin Luther King, Jr. said it much better than I can:

Man cannot save himself, for man is not the measure of all things and humanity is not God. Bound by chains of our own sin and finiteness man needs a Savior. By opening our lives to God in Christ, we become new creatures. *

The only way to break the chains of racism, the only way to tear down that invisible wall, is found in Jesus. That has been my personal experience and the genuine belief of my heart.

MEMORIES AND MORE:

- Tent meetings were once a big deal. This evolved from an even older tradition of "brush arbor" meetings (instead of a tent, the temporary meeting structure was made out of tree branches and brush). Many a church sprang to life out of these meetings. Hundreds of people came to Christ while hearing the message of Jesus preached in tents. It was once a big community event—before attention spans shortened, air conditioning became common, and other options became more attractive and available. Now, tent meetings are rare and more or less a footnote in history, but ask around. I am sure you can still find some folks who remember and may even have been introduced to Christ on a hot, dusty evening sitting in an uncomfortable folding chair under a tent.

- My journey to Lithuania was a God thing. In the fall of 1995, my dear friend and mentor, Dr. Charles F. Myer (or as most knew him—"Bud") and I were at a church growth seminar in Jackson, MS, when he whispered to me the question, "Would you be interested in going to Lithuania for a short-term mission trip?" My response to him was, "Where is that?" Well, I certainly found out and have enjoyed a wonderful relationship with this country and its people ever since.

- Bud Myer (and his wife, Eva) was one of God's unexpected gifts that truly altered my life's course. Bud grew up just across the river from Greenville in McGehee, Arkansas. He was a generation older than me, but that shared geography was one thing we bonded over. He and Eva arrived in Jackson after Bud retired from a career in higher education. They helped me through a difficult stage of my life and opened my world up in numerous ways, including to Lithuania. I am forever thankful for their kind, patient, and generous mentoring and friendship.

- Lithuania is a proud country with a rich history. Once, centuries ago, it boasted a vast European empire. In more recent history, however, it has been at the mercy of other empires—Czarist Russia, Nazi Germany and the Soviet Union. Now, it has come into its own. Vilnius is a beautiful city. The coastal city of Klaipeda is a breath of fresh air. Once, Hitler stood on a balcony overlooking the town center. Now, families pleasantly stroll the streets by the canals, watching ships dock from all over the world. You can find a fantastic castle on an island in the country's center in Trakai. And the lakes—Lithuania is a land of lakes. Every summer, a group from Europe and North America converge on one such lake to enjoy the Baltic Family Camp. Together, we celebrate the bond we share in Jesus—Russians, Lithuanians, Latvians, Estonians, Ukrainians, Czechs, Canadians, Indians, Dutch, Swiss, British, Poles, Germans, Belarussians, and Americans. Christ has totally destroyed any walls of hostility between us. We are family. This is what Jesus does.

- During the events that followed the tragic shooting of the young man on our campus, I witnessed an incredible act of grace and gentle strength that immediately shut down a potentially volatile situation. A large crowd had gathered in our church gym. The temperature outside was beyond frigid, and on the nights that followed the shooting, we invited folks inside. On one occasion, someone produced a portable megaphone and began trying to incite the crowd against the police. Rumors were floating around that some present had guns. For a brief moment, we did not know what to expect. Tensions were heating up. I stood next to some of Levy's leaders, Melvin Hood and Bill Arnold, who nervously wondered, "What should we do?" I think my reply was a lousy attempt at humor, saying, "I don't know. This was never covered in graduate school." Into this, though, stepped the grandmother of the slain young man. She worshiped in a Church of Christ in Little Rock—across the river from us. This eloquent lady approached the megaphone speaker and whispered something to him, and it was all over. The tension vanished, and everyone relaxed again. I do not know what she said, but whatever it was—these are the words we should be speaking to one another: calming words, voices of reason, words that can bring us together instead of keeping us apart.

- I was also impressed at this young man's funeral. Our church at Levy hosted it. The capacity of our sanctuary is perhaps 1000, and we were straining to seat everyone that day. Several area ministers, all preachers from Churches of Christ, participated in officiating. They focused on Jesus. The last and senior minister among the speakers especially brought everyone to the cross of Christ, calling upon us to allow Christ to lead us through such terrible events and turbulent times. I greatly appreciated that emphasis and, of course, wholeheartedly agree.

- Increasingly, it is incredibly challenging to hold on to the middle ground. We discovered that during the days that followed the young man's death when, we heard from people with opinions from all sides. Politically, the extreme voices seem not just to be the loudest but who carry the day. At Levy, we received criticism for not participating in a more significant way in a Black Lives Matter parade only shortly later to hear from critics when one of our shepherds (a white man who adopted a black Haitian son) said in a sermon that yes, in fact, black lives do matter. To me, it seems that we often fail to listen to each other now. That we come into whatever the conversation is with minds firmly made up, along with bullet points to fortify our positions and dismiss anything or anyone who disagrees. And if you are caught in the middle —trying to relate to both sides—watch out! Jesus is described in Scripture as our "mediator" (Hebrews 9:15). Perhaps if we gave him a chance to truly stand in our middle ground, healing instead of hate could break out.

*From "How Should a Christian View Communism," recorded in *Strength to Love*, Harper & Row, 1963. New edition published 2010 by Fortress Press

9

Real Racial Reconciliation

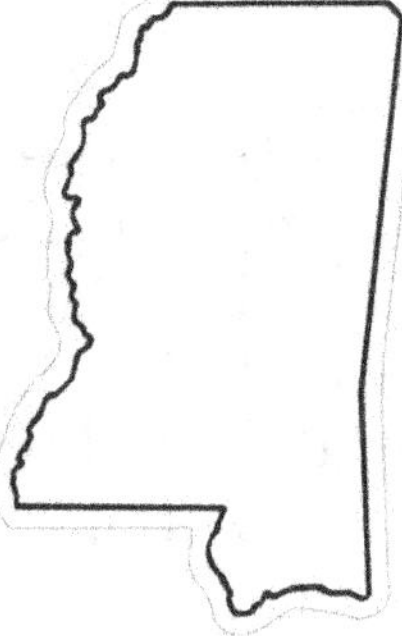

Why would anyone believe that only Jesus can bring about genuine racial reconciliation? After all, for generations, folks who claimed Jesus not only disregarded racism but were often complicit in it. That is certainly true in the history of the Christian church in America. And it is past time that we admit, confess—and yes, repent that we badly missed the mark. We did, but not Jesus. Jesus was way ahead of the curve here. In one sense, his ministry and message were all about racial reconciliation.

First, consider God's original vision for his people to be a community of faith consisting of "every nation, tribe, people and language" (Revelation 7:9; Daniel 7:14; Isaiah 2:2-4). Even as he formed his covenant with the Jewish nation, he desired they be "light for the Gentiles" (Isaiah 42:6). The "light" that was to be shown included honoring justice, mercy, and righteousness for all (Proverbs 31:8-9; Amos 5:24; Micah 6:8; James 1:27—to list a few). Fast forward to Christ's day. His purpose was to extend this light, and God's covenant promises to *everyone* from all nations. The Bible describes it as God's "eternal purpose which he accomplished in Christ Jesus our Lord" (see Ephesians 3:7-11). But nowhere in the Bible does it say it would be easy.

THE SAMARITANS

The world of first-century Palestine was quite the tinderbox (that remains unchanged). Tensions ran high between the orthodox Jewish community and the occupying Roman government. Some (known as "zealots") adopted terrorist tactics in efforts to overthrow Roman rule. Adding to this resentment was the common Jewish disdain for anyone and anything not orthodox, that is, people of other races who had different religious traditions and customs. To most Jews, these outsiders were unclean (due to not complying with the covenantal teaching on ceremonial washing along with other hygiene and dietary-related Jewish legal requirements). They were to be avoided as much as possible. One group of folks in particular felt the prejudicial wrath of the Jews—the Samaritans.

Generations before, they had taken up residence in an area between two thoroughly Jewish regions, Judea and Galilee. Such was the revulsion many Jews felt towards them that when traveling between Judea and Galilee, they would avoid Samaria altogether—taking extreme measures by going many miles out of their way by twice crossing the Jordan River to complete their journey. These racist feelings were generational and ran deep.

Into all of this mix came Jesus. Into this Jewish nationalism, into the protests, violence, and racial tension, into a world filled with hostility, divided by identity and politics, a world defined by all kinds of walls—both visible and invisible. Sound familiar?

And in what He said and did, I see hope and healing, even now, even for us. His teachings were not overtly political, yet they can profoundly affect any political system. The mighty Roman Empire eventually discovered this as the ethos of loving your neighbor and your enemies, going the extra mile, turning the other cheek, and praying for your persecutors proved to be an unstoppable force for change. Jesus spoke directly to the racial tension of his time.

If you have heard of the Samaritans, it is likely due to Jesus. He mentioned them frequently. He made them the heroes of his stories. He intentionally traveled into and through Samaria—not around it. It was the Good Samaritan who helped the bleeding man in the ditch after this helpless victim was ignored by the Jewish elite (Luke 10:25-37). The Samaritan leper alone returned to thank Jesus for being healed, while the other cured nine (all Jewish) did not (Luke 17:11-19). It was a wretched social outcast that Jesus met at a well in Samaria who became the focus of bringing an entire community to faith (John 4). Jesus completely recast the Samaritans, and he did so to puncture both the pride and prejudice of the Jews.

There was no other way for God's will of a multi-ethnic community of faith to occur. Jesus came to provide a path forward for it to happen. His Samaritan emphasis was one way to message it. Even as he was about to ascend heavenward after his resurrection, he informed his disciples to keep spreading the Good News of salvation for all people by directing them to start where they were in Judea but then go next to Samaria and then to the rest of the world (Acts 1:8).

Samaria—the second stop on the way to sharing God's message to the world! That sounded about as unbelievable as having a Jewish Zealot and a Roman tax collector working together on your team, but that was Jesus—intentionally pushing back against the prejudice of his day. He challenged the Jews to tear down their walls of racism, and it cost him his life. It was never going to be easy. Tearing down walls is a tough job.

JESUS DEMOLISHED THE WALL

However, the price Jesus paid only demonstrates the significance of his goal of reconciliation. His sacrifice, combined with the amazing power of the resurrection, offered the Jews then and his followers now an opportunity to reset, to truly reflect the eternal will of God. Here is how the Bible states it:

Christ is the reason we are now at peace. He made us Jews and you who are not Jews one people. We were separated by a wall of hate that stood between us, but Christ broke down that wall. By giving his own body, Christ ended the law with its many commands and rules. His purpose was to make the two groups become one in him. By doing this, he would make peace. (Ephesians 2:14-15 ERV)

These verses are part of a larger amazing text recognizing the work of Jesus as the way to racial healing—for the Jews and non-Jews and for black and white. Through him, by genuinely taking to heart his teachings, being truly remade in his image, and fully claiming a new identity, we can begin the real work of tearing down that wall of hate and hostility. It is fulfilling God's eternal vision of becoming one people in him. But accomplishing this—as said before—takes endurance and a diligent, intentional effort.

ONE MAN'S MISSION OF RACIAL RECONCILIATION

Remember that missive to take the gospel to Samaria and the rest of the world? Well, they did. We see it playing out in the New Testament book of Acts. Christians journeyed to city after city in Asia Minor throughout the Roman Empire, sharing Jesus and planting churches. It is a marvelous story but also one fraught with trouble and tension. Christ's message of reconciliation did not entirely sit well with everyone. They were too invested in keeping the walls up.

Again, this is why tearing down the walls of racism will not happen merely through our efforts alone. Racism is too entrenched. Too many exploit it for their agendas. Satan fuels it through accusations and lies. It is embedded into our world, and only by looking outside of our world can we find help and healing.

This was the exact message a man whose life was utterly transformed by Jesus shared with a church imploding because of racism.

First, the man. His name was Saul. In his time and place, he was notable in that he had the attention of very important people and was rising in the ranks of the elite. His business was Judaism, and he excelled at it (Read his statement about this—Philippians 3:5-6). Of the orthodox, he was the most orthodox. Given a mission to root out Christians from among the Jewish ranks in first-century Palestine, he gave every bit of himself to the job by partnering in at least one execution (Acts 8:1). To Saul, Christianity was an abomination—a bastard child of the Jewish faith that needed to be eradicated. He set about to do that without mercy. That is, until he met Jesus. Then everything changed.

His story is recounted three times in the Book of Acts (chapters 9, 22, & 26), perhaps because it was almost unbelievable. Saul, the persecutor of Christians, actually becoming one? Incredible, but true. He also became one of the most effective missionaries of the first century. Transformed by Jesus, including the new name of Paul, his life goal was to share Christ with the world—especially the non-Jewish world. He became Christ's primary instrument to expand God's community into every nation, tribe, people, and language.

So, when he wrote a letter to the churches in the city of Rome to help them navigate the challenges brought on by racist attitudes within that church, he could speak from his personal navigational experiences. His life stood as a witness to the futility of prejudice.

THE 1ˢᵗ CENTURY CHURCH IN ROME

The situation that created the walls of racism in the house churches scattered throughout the imperial city of Rome was unique. Beginning around 49 AD, all Jews were banished from the city by Caesar Claudius. Not much is known about the details, but the expulsion had to do with some disturbance over "Chrestus" or Christ. This would not be surprising to anyone who has ever read the book of Acts since several disturbances within the Jewish community to the message of Jesus are well documented, and this particular banishment is specifically mentioned (Acts 18:2).

This created the circumstances within those churches that eventually led to division along ethnic lines. After five years (and Claudius's death), the banishment was lifted, and the Jews (including those Jews who were Christ followers) were allowed to return. For those Messianic Jews returning to their churches, it was traumatic. It looked nothing like the church they left. Their worship custom and practices were now absent, and they were not happy about it—not happy at all.

Messianic Jews came to Christ from their long history as God's covenanted people. After all, it was their forefathers whom God had chosen to be his people. Their law and prophets had foreshadowed and foretold the coming of Jesus. It was a natural progression to them—from Abraham to Moses to Elijah to Jesus. They brought all of this rich heritage into their faith expressions in Christ. All of it is connected. All of it was meaningful. But much of it was missing when they returned to church in Rome.

Non-Jews came to faith in Christ differently. With no such history to call upon, their faith was not informed by ancient stories or canonized law. They saw hope and healing in Jesus, offering a fresh start and a way out of an empty life with no future. The exciting idea of a faith community working together to make a difference in the world by selflessly serving others stood in stark contrast to the brutal, immoral, and ruthless culture of the Roman world. Their expressions of and journey to faith, therefore, were different than the Jews. And they had been there for five years following and worshipping Jesus through these decidedly non-Jewish approaches.

So, the table was set for racial and theological confrontation and tension. And did it ever happen! This is when the Apostle Paul wrote the letter we know as the New Testament book of Romans. It is in this letter that I see how we can arrive at real racial conciliation.

NONE ARE RIGHTEOUS

From the start, by reading this letter, you can capture the tenseness of the situation. The dispute along ethnic lines over what the church should look like had erupted into finger-pointing, accusations, and passing judgment (See chapters 1-2). Jews thought their DNA and history with God offered them elite status. The non-Jews thought their faith purer—not hindered by the burden of Jewish law. The fight was on, church be damned! It was not a good look for a community that was supposed to be for *all people*. So, Paul set out to correct and bring them back into the focus of Christ.

He begins by indicting them all by reminding them of their faults. How could they judge someone else, he stated, while doing the same things? None had any high moral ground to stand on. Actually, without Jesus, they were all just a bunch of sinners and worthy of God's judgment. "There is none righteous, no not one," he proclaimed (Romans 3:23). This was and is a crucial point. Regardless of who we think we are, what our DNA may be, what kind of elite status we may claim, and what privileges we believe we are entitled to, Paul proclaims—outside of Jesus, none of it matters. We are all on the same sinking ship of sin, and it will not matter then; if we are in first class or steerage, the same sea will rise to claim us all. Only Jesus can save us. Now, if we can all figure out a way to start here together and allow Jesus to raise us up, there is no wall anywhere that will be able to resist.

After taking them through spiritual boot camp, he extends a great deal of effort demonstrating from Old Testament Scripture and stories how it was always God's will and desire for his community to include both Jews and non-Jews—everyone from all nations, tribes, peoples, and languages! Christianity was never meant to be based on ethnicity. Abraham—the "Father of the Jews," is actually the father of all who come to faith in Christ. And while it is true that God had a special relationship with the Jewish people, whom Paul compares to a cultivated olive tree, he always had in mind the others. Christ brought the others (Samaritans! Us!) in as a "wild olive branch" engrafted into that long-nurtured olive tree. Now, both the new branch and the existing tree are nourished together by God. All belong. All have a place and a purpose in Jesus (see chapters 4-11).

How can this inform us in the twenty-first century as we deal with the ongoing challenge of race and consider ways to tear down that wall? After all, we are a long, long way from that Jew/non-Jew situation in ancient Rome. Or are we?

TRANSFORMATION

Consider what Paul does next. Starting in Romans 12,

he switches gears—putting the practical into the theological. And it is right at this point where we find our help. Here are his words:

Therefore, I urge you, in view of God's mercy, to offer yourselves as living sacrifices, holy and pleasing to God—this is your spiritual act of worship. Do not conform any longer to the pattern of this world, but be transformed by the renewing of your mind. Then you will be able to test and approve what God's will is—his good and perfect will. (Romans 12:1-2)

Three distinct disciplines are being called for in this text. Three, which, if embodied and practiced, will tear down the *invisible walls* of racism, prejudice, pride, and whatever else helps create and build these walls.

First, it is the discipline of self-sacrifice. This is a common theme in the call to Christ. It is the loss of self for the gain of Christ and his blessing. Jesus spoke of it in terms of "the first being last and the last being first" (Matthew 20:16). It is an inverted way of thinking compared to almost every culture. It leads to, incredibly enough, doing "nothing out of selfish ambition" but instead considering "others better than yourselves" (See Philippians 2:3-5). Jesus embodied self-sacrifice, literally dying to make reconciliation possible. We can easily see the need for selflessness in the Roman church context, but also in our own. If we could ever grow to this point, whatever walls we have erected toward others will begin to crumble. It is not easy, but it is achievable in Jesus.

Next, remember how I have mentioned my lack of faith in any political solution to racism and racial injustice? Recall when I stated that by and through our abilities, we will not solve this problem. Here is the reason and the second point. That is the pattern of the world. This is

Satan's domain, and he is most definitely not about any reconciliation. It is that clichéd definition of crazy: "Keep doing the same things repeatedly while expecting a different outcome." That is our history when it comes to race. Paul realized the Roman Christians' bickering and race-baiting approach had to go—absolutely no path forward to healing was found there. Conforming to that pattern was a dead end. How true this continues to be. Can we see that? After years of trying and failing to demolish racist walls, shouldn't we consider another way? This is why Paul would state in another letter to another church, "From now on, we regard no one from a worldly point of view" (2 Corinthians 5:16).

Shouldn't we consider the transformed way? Transformation! This is the third directive of the text. Paul could personally speak into that! He had everything changed in Jesus. From persecutor to preacher, from elitist to evangelist, from racist to rescuer, he left the pattern of the world in his dust in re-making himself in the image of Christ. It is about a new identity—one free from the constraints, limitations, prejudices, and suspicions of the old. Consider all of the "new" language at play in the New Testament: becoming a "new creature" (2 Corinthians 5:17); being "born again" (John 3:3); taking off the old man and putting on the new (Romans 6:3-5); and being "clothed with Christ" (Galatians 3:27). No longer is our primary identity skin color or political affiliation or any other wall-creating iteration. Can we do this? Dare we do this? How do we do this? Let's try something new!

ACCEPT ONE ANOTHER

Let's get back to Paul's message to the Roman Christians. He gets down to it (please read Romans 12:1-15:7 for his entire message) in the most practical way: addressing what transformation looks like in their context and how, ultimately, if they do it, they will find the path in Christ of complete acceptance of one another.

How to get there? It is no accident that he starts by asking them to get over themselves. "Don't think of yourself more highly than you should" is precisely how it puts it. That would begin to solve a lot. Next, he stresses the need to understand that differences can be good. No one is alike, and that is not just okay but preferred because we all can serve Jesus through our personalities and giftedness. We can actually celebrate our diversity instead of feeling threatened by it.

The charge to "Be devoted to one another in love" follows. Linger over those words. Both devotion and love are wall demolishers. Hospitality comes into play. What if we all decided to invite people of different colors and backgrounds into our homes and spend time with them to know better, understand, and appreciate them? Next, he begins a thread that runs throughout the text—be dedicated to peace—not vengeance or judgment or anything else that would destroy the joy and harmony found in Christ. Do what promotes peace and mutual encouragement in the faith community and the larger community, not what purposefully harms it.

Love, he says, does no harm to anyone. *Full stop here.* It is not the will of Christ to harm, divide, or antagonize, nor should it be that of his followers, regardless of provocation, political posturing, or even blatant social injustice. Love simply does not harm. It is not violent. Period. No exceptions. It seeks solutions. It is always about reconciliation even when and where differences occur—we should respect one another in those differences. This is the way of transformation. This tears down the wall.

And the basis for doing this? Again, it will not come from the pattern of the world. Accusations will not lead us down this healing path. Washington, D.C., will not be able to legislate into anyone's heart. It will not flow out of our magnanimous efforts. We will only learn it and do it one way.

"Accept one another then, just as Christ accepted you."

There it is. If walls are ever to fall, If racial prejudice is ever to be eradicated, If we ever hope to heal as a people, as a nation, this is how we will do it. I will accept you not based on skin color, socio-economic status, gender, zip code, political persuasion, voting record, or because I have a star on my belly (for all of you Dr. Suess fans), but because Jesus accepted me. See, he values none of those constructs. He values us just as we are and the faith that brought us to him. There are no artificial walls with him. Even though we are solidly on team, "none righteous, no not one" and undeserving of it, he loves, accepts, and forgives us anyway. It is called *grace.* If he can accept me, then who am I not to accept, love, and forgive you—even if you are from Samaria?

Grace destroys the hate, pride, prejudice, and anger that fuels racism. Grace forgives. Grace offers a chance to reset, restart, and renew. Grace brings about reconciliation with no more walls separating us.

Is that possible, or is it just a pipe dream? If we believe what the Bible says and in the power of Jesus, then yes, because "with God all things are possible" (Matthew 19:26). And even if we doubt that, what else has worked?

It takes me back to my childhood. Ole Mose offering his rough, but gentile hand to a frightened kid. Taking that fear away and turning it into a friendship—accepting one another just as we were. Tearing down that wall between us. Or to Hoss, who patiently put up with me when he could have just as quickly dismissed me. Or to Clay, who eventually made his dent in the wall. The question for us now is, can we set aside our self-serving agendas, identity emphasis, and entrenched conclusions to make that happen now? Can we make it not about ourselves and rise above our differences, give Christ a chance to work and come together in him to seek lasting solutions and genuine racial reconciliation?

I believe we can, but only in Jesus. Jesus is the forever wall-breaker.

MEMORIES AND MORE:

- Bible geography. Whew. I barely made it through this class at Magnolia Bible College— all those ancient, faraway spots on a map. Even now, it can be challenging, but it also brings life to Bible stories. Go check out a map of Palestine in the first century. Find the Jordan River. Locate Jerusalem in the region of Judea. Look north and find Galilee. Next, discover Samaria in the middle. You will then begin to see how deeply entrenched the hatred and prejudice Jews felt toward the Samaritans. They added hours and miles when traveling from Nazareth to Jerusalem by avoiding Samaria.
- One way Jesus smashed walls was by having both a tax collector (Matthew, who would have rightly been seen as an agent for the occupying Roman government) and a Zealot (Simon, a

terrorist dedicated to overthrowing that government) on his team. Both became Apostles through Jesus's transforming healing power. If these two sworn enemies found reconciliation in Jesus, anyone can.

- We know of the "Chrestus" problem in Rome through the Jewish historian Suetonius in his *Lives of the Twelve Caesars.* Here, he mentions the growing Christian presence in the empire and notes the Jewish expulsion from the city of Rome. However, there remains debate if "Chrestus" is a direct reference to Christ.

- The Apostle Paul was an incredible man, the perfect person to bridge the gap between Jewish and non-Jewish Christ followers. There are volumes of books dedicated to his life. Of course, the New Testament book of Acts is the place to start. A friend, Tom Kloske, recently wrote another excellent, easy-to-read resource. It is entitled *The Astonishing and Daunting Journeys of the Apostle Paul.* I recommend it!

- *The Sneetches and Other Stories* is a terrific book by the indomitable Dr. Suess. In it, he punctures prejudice by telling the tale of the Sneetches and their ultimate decision to accept one another regardless. It all had to do with "stars on thars." As he told it, some Sneetches had stars on their bellies. Some did not. Those with stars thought themselves superior and had star-belly privilege. The star-less Sneetches suffered. Into this came an enterprising fellow who had a star-making machine. For a small fee, all Sneetches could have "stars on thars." This would have brought equality, but it was not to be. The original Star Belly Sneetches would have none of it. So, this entrepreneur developed a star-removing technique. Off came the stars! And so it went until none of the Sneetches could even discern who was who. Finally, they decided how ridiculous it was, forgot about it, and accepted each other as is. This fable can still inform us. Racism is ridiculous, and there is always someone around waiting to exploit it for profit.

- One more wall-breaking statement from the book of Romans: "Each of us should please his neighbor for his own good, to build him up" (15:2). Reminiscent of the Golden Rule, imagine what could happen if we all put this into practice? It flows from another uniquely Jesus trait—it is not about me! Racism makes everything about me, but Jesus makes it about others, and that is a game changer. "For even Jesus did not please himself" (the next verse, Romans 15:3). How else will we learn to accept one another?

Epilogue

Not only do I believe that accepting one another as Jesus teaches can happen and then lead to racial reconciliation, but it already has. I take you back to my home state of Mississippi. In the general proximity of some of the most tragic civil rights atrocities in our country and literally in the shadow of Civil War history sits a Church of Christ on a bypass highway in Vicksburg, MS.

Vicksburg is a charming, small southern town on the banks and bluffs of the Mississippi River—not too far down that river from my hometown of Greenville. History seeps out of the red clay soil there. Almost everywhere you look on the town's hills are reminders of the Civil War. From May 18 to July 4, 1863, the Union Army laid siege to fortress Vicksburg. Before this, this Confederate stronghold had thwarted and prevented all Federal attempts to break the river blockade and gain full access to the entirety of the mighty Mississippi. The siege, however, did the trick—starving out both military and civilian. Ulysses S. Grant cemented his reputation during this battle, moving on to bigger and better posts. In some ways, this battle still defines Vicksburg, with the beautiful national park tracing the battle lines along with monuments from the states that sent troops to fight and die there. In addition to this battlefield, the old courthouse museum recounts the area's rich history. Coca-Cola was first bottled in a drug store in Vicksburg in 1894. There is a museum for that, too.

I always enjoy visiting Vicksburg. Growing up, we traveled there occasionally to see relatives, the Barefoot family (their name always fascinated me as a kid). I still recoil, remembering an out-of-control bike ride down one of those impossibly steep heels that resulted in a crash and scrapped knee. I've spent hours in the military park imagining that human struggle while hearing echoes off in the distance of the last gasps of the Old South. I experienced my first-ever indoor shopping mall in Vicksburg. The Battlefield Mall made such an impression that I can still recall it in amazing detail. When I get the rare opportunity to stop in now, I always try to do so at lunchtime to eat at Walnut Hills. It is an old antebellum-type house converted into a restaurant serving the delicious southern fried taste of Mississippi—exactly my kind of food.

But there is another reason why Vicksburg stands out. My friend, college classmate, preacher, and educator, Dr. Willie Nettle, planted the Bypass Church of Christ (Obviously located on a bypass—remember I mentioned earlier how we have little imagination in naming our congregations) in the 1980s and has remained there effectively leading this community of faith ever since. Willie is black, as is some of his church, but not nearly all of it. Several years ago, the Bypass church successfully merged with a white congregation. They are fully integrated with black and white staff and elders.

Now, certainly, and thankfully, there are many fully integrated congregations across our land. Still, very few intentionally came together while maintaining the equality seen in the Bypass Church, especially this far in the deep South. Willie will be the first to deflect any praise and give all the glory to God. He will also be the first to admit that it was not easy. It did not happen by following the pattern of the world. Grace was the key to the transformation. They had to overcome old, stubborn, comfortable racial stereotypes and latent racism and learn to accept each other as Christ had accepted them. The walls eventually came down, and a thriving, multi-ethnic, peaceful church of every nation, tribe, people, and language emerged. As a result, not only are they a light shining on a hill (both literally and figuratively), but they are the hands and feet of Jesus to the city, working to share Jesus with all, but especially the homeless community, in a beautiful way through their Living Lives Family Shelter ministry.

Talking to Willie now, he will also tell you that, yes, on occasion, they have to continue the dialogue. His folks watch the news, too, and the panic, the fear, the anger that still springs from the accuser can creep back in an attempt to lay bricks back up on that wall. But they refuse to allow that to happen. Instead, they persevere, encouraging others to follow their example. Inviting others to find those pathways in Jesus that demolish all walls—all within the shadow of that history. Racism itself will never end, but we can *demolish the walls* it has created between us.

You are all children of God through faith in Christ Jesus, for all of you who were baptized into Christ have clothed yourself with Christ. There is neither Jew nor Greek, slave nor free, male nor female, for you are all one in Christ Jesus. (Galatians 3:26-28)

Acknowledgments

I greatly appreciate Aretha "Faye" Dodson and Eva Walker Myer's contributions to this book. Their perspective, input, editing, and support were invaluable to me. It was a long time coming, so thank you!

About the Author

"You can take the boy out of the Delta, but you can never take the Delta out of the boy." This is true for Danny Dodd. After growing up in Greenville, MS, Danny has spent his life in ministry within Churches of Christ across the South and the globe, serving in churches in Louisiana, Mississippi, Florida, Arkansas, and the European country of Lithuania. Still, his Mississippi roots remain ever with him.

He is a husband and father. He married Terri in 2000 and has three beautiful daughters, Natalie, Taylor, and Jordan. Danny is the preaching minister for the Levy Church of Christ in North Little Rock, AR.

For more of Danny's writings, please visit his blog, *Adventures in Preaching* at https://dannydodd.wordpress.com/

Also by Danny Dodd

Revelation is Relevant

God, Government and Us